LEARNING TO DRIVE INTO THE NOW

INTO THE NOW

PRND

Solan McClean

LEARNING TO DRIVE INTO THE NOW

Welcome to Learning to Drive: PRND! This book is the culmination of many hours of practice development and experience. I have tried to put down in words what can only be experienced by each of us as individuals.

The practices and techniques described in this book can help you change your life, open up to your higher self, and realize the truth about your own egoic thinking. I urge you to be open to putting these ideas into practice in your own life to clear away the veil of ego and transform your way of living.

I have learned only through experience. I have read a lot of self-help books and articles over the years and have gotten a lot of good concepts, ideas, and exercises from that material. I have only kept that which has proven itself under the scrutiny of direct experience. Like the Buddha said…try it out, if it's for you, keep it. If it doesn't work for you, discard it.

So I have arrived at this moment…the jumping off point of writing down my ideas about how to live a conscious, fulfilled, awake life. A journey of being using the experience and the analogy of driving your car as the vehicle because it is so simple, yet revealing to each of us as individuals. It is my hope that you can put some of what you read here to the test, and hopefully, if it works for you, keep it.

TABLE OF CONTENTS

CHAPTER 1

OUR CARS...OURSELVES

*"Truth is the same always. Whoever ponders it will get the
same answer. Buddha got it. Patanjali got it. Jesus got it.
Mohammed got it. The answer is the same, but the method
of working it out may vary this way or that. "*

— **Swami Satchidananda**

In my many years of driving, I've noticed that my car is really an
extension of my physical self and to a large degree, a very revealing part of my mental self, or the way I think and behave. If I am
in a bad mood, I tend to drive more aggressively. If I am feeling
tranquil, I am more apt to drive closer to the posted speed limit
and be far more courteous to other drivers.

Since learning to drive at the age of sixteen, I quickly had to
develop a sense of the physical boundaries of the car I was driving. If I were backing up, I had to have an approximate idea in my
mind's eye of where the back bumper of the car was so I didn't hit
the trash cans. While traveling down the interstate, I had to be

aware of the proximity of the width of my car as I passed by others in the lanes next to me. I especially needed that keen awareness of the outside perimeter of the metal that made up my car when threading the needle between concrete road construction barriers or when sandwiched between two tractor trailers.

After a few months, these spatial awareness's became second nature and I was able to navigate the challenges of driving anywhere at any time. I wasn't slowed by rain, road conditions, or even while driving a different type of car. Somewhere in my unconscious, I had made a connection between the physical dimensions of the car and the feel of my own body on the steering wheel, accelerator, and brakes. Just like riding a bike, it became second nature...the mind–body connection. I must admit I had to pay extra attention while driving a big rental truck or oversized pickup, but for the most part, I had learned what almost every American has to learn. I was one with the automobile!

There is a sense of ease when behind the wheel that I think the majority of us feel. I have heard driving referred to as relaxing, invigorating, and just plain fun. Some of us do our best thinking while driving our car. I've heard it exclaimed on more than one occasion that someone was going to go for a drive and "clear their mind." So there is definitely something about the dynamic exercise of getting from point A to point B, or even just aimlessly cruising around, that seems to fit the human condition very well.

Such was the case with me. I fell in love with driving. I will admit that really long road trips were not my bag. But the opportunity to run out and grab something at the store or pick someone up were never lost on me. Add to the experience a great sound system and some favorite music, and we're in for a great time. I also fell in love with the convertible. Why someone would drive a car with a top on it when they didn't have to was beyond me. But to each his own...from the oversized pickup truck to the smallest, fastest, most expensive sports car...there are as many types of vehicles as there are personalities to drive them.

Our cars are very personal to us. They are not only our mode of transportation, they are one of our biggest investments and ongoing expenses. We wash them, vacuum them, wax them, maintain them, show them off, and sometimes live in them. They are our home away from home. They hold not only our belongings but also our memories. We all have fond and maybe not so fond memories of adventures we have taken in our cars. When it's time to get a new car, many of us have felt a twinge of sadness at letting go of our trusted old friend. But like relationships, we move on even as the memory of our old vehicle fades into the past.

When someone compliments our ride, we feel a rush of pride, and when someone pokes fun at our old or not so fresh looking transportation, we can't help but take it personally. So, is it just a car? No. It is an extension of ourselves.

For most of us, driving may be our only time to be truly by ourselves. With families, jobs, and so much to accomplish every day, we find ourselves rushing from person to person and task to task and rarely find time to be truly in a place of solitude. Now you may say, "Solitude? On a busy highway at rush hour?" I say yes—solitude. If we are alone in our vehicle, we have safety, some privacy, the ability to do as we will without being questioned, and a little time to think in an intimately familiar place without having to answer to anyone.

It is during this time that some of us worry the most as we go over what happened earlier in the day, or last week, or last year. We play out fantasies in our mind of future endeavors and outcomes. We plan for eventualities and come to conclusions about schemes that were never even born. We get lost in our thoughts, our music, our books on tape, and many times, our reactions to other drivers around us. Our cars are our rooms, and sometimes the only real personal space we may have in our lives.

It's no wonder that we feel so personally connected to our vehicles and are so emotionally attached to our driving experience. It is with this understanding that the idea for an experiment on myself occurred.

Driven to Distraction

Every year, thousands of people are killed in distracted driving accidents. Although texting or talking on a cell phone while driving is now against the law in most places, people continue this practice despite its well-documented dangers and illegality.

It is the aim of this book to help you develop a focused attention on your driving experience while behind the wheel. Obviously, distractions to driving are detrimental not only to your practice of mindful driving but also to your safety and perhaps your wallet.

This also holds true for other types of driving distractions like grooming or putting on makeup while driving, eating, reading (I know...really?), and fooling with the radio, mp3 player, or other electronics. In the interest of setting a good environment conducive to the development of a mindful driving practice, these habits must be eliminated. Not only do they take your mind off the road, they steal your attention away from your practice of relaxed, mindful awareness of the present moment while on the road.

Take care of all your grooming needs before hitting the road. This may mean getting up a few minutes early to prepare yourself. Make this a part of your practice. Get into your vehicle ready to drive without distraction, and this includes eating. Put your cell phone away or at least face down so you are not tempted to read texts or answer calls until you have arrived at your destination or at least pulled off the road. Keep the music off for now. Hearing the sounds of the road as you drive will become a part of your practice development, especially early on. Later, when you feel you have developed a solid practice, you may want to introduce relaxing, meditative music to the mix. I always avoid talk radio as it is an attention stealer and at the very least, will compete with your practice for your attention.

While you start out on this journey of mindful driving, it is good to observe distractions and either find a way to transcend them or eliminate them completely. It is obviously hard to practice with someone else talking in the car. You can either find a way to drive alone, or focus your attention on your driving experience and do your best to minimize the distraction. If your practice is developed enough, perhaps you can arrive at a happy medium of mindfully engaging the passenger while practicing mindful driving. You really have to relax and find the best way that gives you the clearest practice experience.

❈❈ ❈❈

Road Rage: Let's Make Mindful Driving All the Rage

If you've ever watched an online video channel, chances are you've come across a video of a road rage incident. You see it on the nightly news, in pop culture commentary, and in your local community. The videos range from shouting and flipping drivers off to deadly intentional vehicular assaults and shootings. Why is this? Where did all this rage come from? It is hard to define in any exact terms. I'm sure the reasons are as varied as ourselves.

One thing is for sure. It has got to stop. Road rage is typically born of aggressive driving habits and the mindset that we are separate and in competition with all other drivers on the road. We feel slighted by the actions of another driver and feel the need to take revenge. We feel we are justified in "straightening out" the other driver. Chances are we have all experienced those feelings while on the road. Hopefully, we did not act on them.

Young people are especially susceptible to road rage, so it seems appropriate that defusing the initial feelings that are the beginning of road rage should be taught in driver education programs. Half of all drivers who are on the receiving end of road rage behavior will react with the same vitriol, if not worse, and that number is only increasing.

It is dangerous enough to drive your car on a busy interstate at speeds north of 50 miles per hour without having the additional threat of raging drivers creating an even more dangerous driving environment.

So what would be a good first step? Well…it all begins with you. You have to learn to let it go. If you perceive someone has done you wrong on the road by cutting you off or not letting you into their lane, feel that initial feeling, and then take a deep breath and consciously let it go. You're not only making your own life better and more serene, but you are heading off a possible escalation of road rage. Who knows, maybe the other driver is having a bad day, maybe a death in the family, or they are driving to the emergency room with an injured child. Give them the benefit of the doubt, and you will give yourself the gift of serenity for the rest of the drive. Try it! You'll find yourself smiling silently and thinking about it next time a similar situation arises.

When someone comes after you with road rage it is best to quickly de-escalate the situation by either letting them vent and moving on or mouthing an apology. Believe me, I know how hard it is to resist that natural impulse to give it back to them twice as hard. In the end, it serves no one…especially your higher self. Even if you feel you did nothing wrong, it is far more noble to take the high road and be the bigger person. The more you practice this in your driving, the better you will feel about yourself as a person, and you will have become a much safer driver for all of society. Isn't that reward enough?

Another way to head off potential road rage feelings is to de-stress your driving experience. That is what this book is all about. When you bring about an environment of calm and serenity inside your car, it is much harder to fail to recognize the beginning feelings of road rage and nip those feelings in the bud. If you're driving on a busy street, late and stressed, you are a prime candidate to easily slip into a road rage altercation. If you realize this when you are confronted with a raging driver, you will be able to understand how unfortunate that poor person is. Observe their behavior and it will allow you to understand that those feelings are toxic and dangerous, and you have no need for them in your life, let alone your driving.

A key ingredient for a safer, calmer driving experience is relaxation. Diminishing stress and deactivating old reactive patterns when practicing mindful driving can really change not only your driving experience, but your living experience. The tools we put into practice in the car make their way into life outside your vehicle, too. How? Experience! When you find out that you can have that serene feeling of being less stressed and have an overall calmer demeanor while practicing your driving, you will naturally seek out that same serenity everywhere in the outside world. This is one of the secrets to the practice. As it manifests itself in your experiential makeup, you will notice a use for it in all aspects of your life. What a blessing it can be!

So please, read on, share what you learn. You too can help to de-stress the driving population and decrease the amount of road rage that is plaguing our nation's roads.

You may be thinking "But I already drive…why would I learn to do something I already know how to do?"

While I am assuming the vast majority of readers are already drivers, I should make it clear that I am not advocating that you learn to drive all over again. Just that you learn how to drive differently. How differently is up to you and your personal set of beliefs of how these ideas and exercises can change your life for the better. Maybe one single change in the way you think about yourself behind the wheel can make your life a few percentage points better. But isn't that totally worth the effort?

We all know the rules of the road as spelled out in our particular state's traffic code. But what about our *personal* traffic code. I remember when seat belt laws went into effect in my state. Prior to that safety practice becoming the rule of law, I very seldom, if ever, wore my seat belt. I thought it would be uncomfortable, and I rationalized my safety concern with some anecdotal story I had heard from some vague source about how someone could have survived their horrific crash if they had only **not** been wearing their seat belt. *See*, I told myself, *seat belts can kill!*

At first, I felt as though it was a violation of my God-given rights to require me to wear a seat belt in the personal confines of my car. (Another example of how we personalize our cars and our driving experience.) It was, after all, my car and my body… therefore, my decision. Right? Stories began to emerge of traffic stops and hefty fines being levied for not wearing your "safety harness," so I eventually accepted and capitulated to the law. It wasn't long before I realized it was probably one of the best safety laws ever enacted and wondered why it wasn't instituted sooner. And guess what? I now feel uncomfortable if my seat belt is not on!

What I am going to suggest in the following chapters is that you be at least open to trying a few of the ideas set forth in this book, the aim of which is to not only enrich your driving experience, but through that experience, enrich your life outside of your car. Let me give you one quick example.

One of the best decisions I ever made was to start driving with a sense of compassion toward other drivers…particularly the ones whom I considered bad drivers. No lane change signal, not moving out of the passing lane while going slower than everyone else, waiting till the last minute to squeeze into the single lane in a construction zone. You know the type. The ones I usually yelled at, flipped off, and honked at.

So, one day I decided to try to be cooperative and courteous to especially those wretched souls of the road...and guess what? It literally made me laugh out loud! That's right, full on LOL! I was only on the highway about two minutes when I spotted a car in my rearview mirror coming up on my right at a high rate of speed. I noticed that the car in front of him (which was next to me) was going about the same speed as me. He came up behind that car and was riding his bumper, so I knew he really must be in a hurry. I thought to myself, the old me would have boxed this joker in and reveled in the fact that he was getting payback for being an unsafe jerk. Would that have made for a safer situation? No. It actually would have made for a more dangerous one. But I thought about what I would feel. I would get that sense of satisfaction that I was putting a jerk in his place. But I know that deep down, it puts me in the same place as that jerk. What if he was late to pick up his child at school? What if he was on his way to help his sick mother who had fallen (and couldn't get up)?

Although I would never know his reason for being in a hurry, I decided to give him the benefit of the doubt and actually help him on his way. I slowed down and dropped back in my lane, giving him a clear shot to pass and be on his way. He immediately took the opening and sped on past the car that had been in front of him. What did it cost me? Nothing.

As he shot past me, I looked over and nodded to him. He didn't even look over at me. It made me smile at first. Then I started laughing. It felt so strange to actually help someone pass me and be on their way. Someone I didn't know and probably never would. Someone whose circumstances I would never realize and didn't even care to know. As I laughed, I realized that it actually felt really good to be in control of the situation and help someone else out.

Helping people feels good! Even if it might be someone who is just an aggressive driver or a jerk on the road. I definitely helped out the driver in front of him. I alleviated the danger of having a car riding his back bumper. I was a hero of the road. So simple and so entertaining for myself. It felt like a win/win!

Oddly enough, I carried that feeling to the grocery store with me as I got out of my car and grabbed a cart. I took one from the cart return and walked it back into the store. Normally, I would have walked right past those carts. It wasn't my job to bring them back in. That's what my purchase money goes for. But with my newfound feeling of cooperation, I thought, *It's one less cart to deal with for the high school kid who's working here part time, and I'm going that way anyway.* And guess what? It felt good—only to me, and only right then—but isn't that what life really is? One moment at a time? Why not make that moment the best moment I can? Simple things. Right?

I walked into the store feeling good when I might have walked in feeling tense, or bored, or even aggravated by the behavior of the driver I had just encountered on the highway. It felt good to cooperate with the world. It is my hope that you too can feel just a little bit better, a little more at ease, and a little more compassionate. Learn to drive in a better way, and you can learn to live a little bit better too. You have nothing to lose, and the upside is pretty darn good.

⚊◅⊹ ⊹▻⚊

Learning to Live in the Moment

By learning to drive in a mindful and fully conscious way, we can develop our driving practice to be cooperative and compassionate. So what happens to us when we are "mindful" or "fully conscious?"

Well, that is really the question of the day, isn't it? The answer, I'm afraid is actually nothing. Nothing happens all that differently in our world. We are in the same location, set of circumstances, and the same relationships. We have the same home, job, finances, problems, and blessings.

The difference comes not from any "thing," but from a change in the way we perceive our life. That is, in the current moment. Most of us live our lives always spending more time focused on the future or the past, imagining outcomes or scenarios that don't yet exist, or reliving events from the past and experiencing the corresponding emotions that memories can bring. The point is that we are missing the reality of the present moment...the only true life we will ever have. Once we are able to plug our attention back into experiencing the actual moment—the life we are living—we connect in a way that is full, astonishing, and transcendent. We are not transcending the world, our environment, our bodies, or anything else that exists in the physical world. We are transcending ourselves...that is, our egoic mind or what we have believed to be ourselves.

When past and future take over our attention, those thoughts and mental images are mistaken for our reality. We lose contact with what is actually real...this moment in our life. We are led down false paths by our egoic mind. Fantasy and memory are taken as who we are, and we suffer the emotional confusion and anxiety that goes along with being disconnected from our real essence, our true self. Once you realize your true self can only be experienced in the current moment, you are on the road to living the truth.

Your practice becomes an experience of being in the moment without the filter of the egoic mind. You practice pure presence. You move through the world unattached by the mental conditioning you have acquired in your lifetime. Judgment, emotional reaction, categorizing, and anxiety subside when confronted with the truth of the present moment. The result is a more peaceful mind, relaxed body, and calmer demeanor. This usually leads to better decision making, more compassion toward others and ourselves, and a real connection to everyone and everything in the world. If you've ever heard the expression, "Get your butt into gear," now is the time. Put your life into drive.

If this sounds too good to be true…it isn't. Practice, and find out for yourself.

CHAPTER 2

MUMBO JUMBO VS. HOCUS POCUS

"Mind is a flexible mirror, adjust it, to see a better world."

— Amit Ray

Now I suppose you are ready to hear about some really wild, out-there, esoteric trip about how you can find yourself by following some magic steps, incantations, chants, and by worshipping yet another god or guru...this is not the case.

But if that helps you pay attention to the present moment, use it! You may be thinking, "Not another 'present moment' guy!" You may have read Ram Dass or Eckhart Tolle and be thinking, "I already read this stuff, and although it made sense to me, it was really hard to make it work in any meaningful way in my life." Well, that is where Learning to Drive comes in. You will learn to put the present moment at the forefront of your time spent behind the wheel.

I remember never having meaningful time to sit down in a quiet place for any amount of time to meditate. Guess what happened? I couldn't put together a meaningful practice, so it didn't come to fruition for me. That doesn't mean it doesn't work. In fact, at one time, I did make the time, and it worked quite well. All it means is that my priorities were not in line with what I wanted to achieve through the practice of quiet, sitting meditation. So it didn't work for me—at that time.

I noticed when I decided to practice mindfulness while driving that it was a good fit because I was in my car several times a day and usually alone. I was used to zoning out to music and thoughts in my head while I drove, so I felt my time could be better spent. My thoughts usually drove me to agitation and anxiety anyway, so I was not really giving up much. If you are the same, this can be a really great thing for you. If not…it can still be a really great thing for you.

Here is what you need to know:

- It is not magic
- It is not religion
- It is not brainwashing
- It will make gradual changes in your way of thinking
- The change will be slow or nonexistent at times and like a lightning bolt at other times
- If nothing else…it will make you a better, more compassionate driver
- It can bring you a little more peace and serenity than you have in your life right now

With that said, you may be asking, "That's great…but how does this fit with my religious beliefs (or maybe my atheism)?" The fact is that it fits with none of it and all of it. It is not a replacement for your religious beliefs. In fact, it can bring you a deeper connection with your spiritual being no matter how your mind perceives your God, Goddess, or Higher Power. If you believe that we are all there is and there is no God, that's fine too. It will be a great experiment for you to get in deeper touch with you. The side of you that feels creativity and life directly, without the filter of the thinking mind. That's a pretty good upside for trying out something that doesn't require you to make extra time to do it.

You may also be thinking, "OK. What's the first step?" If you're asking that question, you've already taken it. The first step is just to be open to the idea that trying out the process of mindfulness (or rather mindlessness, as we shall discuss) while driving is worth the effort if it can bring about even a small positive change in your life.

All we are seeking to do is to use the experience of driving your car to learn how to quiet the thinking (egoic) mind and open up the compassionate self (the Real You) that lies beneath everything you think and do. I suspect that once you make contact with "the Real You," you are going to want more. Our "real" self is someone we always felt we could be but could never quite hang onto. We caught glimpses. When we helped someone in need, when we did the right thing even though no one was watching, or when we taught someone something that made their life better. The only thing standing in the way of you being the Real You is your egoic mind.

Here's where the mumbo jumbo and the hocus pocus meet the road. "What do you mean? There are two of me?" Well, actually, yes. You can't see them, but they are there. One is real. One is not. If you've ever heard of the duality of man or the story of the garden of Eden, you will know what I am talking about. Adam and Eve lived in bliss until they discovered what they perceived as good and evil. Only their analytical thinking could discern between what they desired and what they sought to avoid. It is a mechanism built into each one of us…it helps us to learn to survive. So how can this be bad? It's not. It is required. It is when we *identify* with that part of ourselves so much that we believe it is who we actually are that causes problems. A collection of likes and dislikes, positives and negatives, good and bad…judgments.

I'm sure you've experienced a situation where something happened and you thought it was the worst thing in the world. How could this happen to me? I will never be the same. Only you came to discover later that it was a blessing. I lost my job and then I got a better one. My relationship failed, and then I found someone new who fits my life better. Maybe these things happen for a reason. The point is, we don't know from minute to minute where we stand. Why? Because life is dynamic. Nothing stays the same. Life is in constant flux. What a recipe for confusion and anxiety, right? It can be if you live your life identified with only your egoic mind.

It is here where some salvation can be found. The Real You, or the spiritual you, or the compassionate you, or whatever you would like to call it has a way of knowing and calming. Some refer to it as your gut, your instinct, or your unspoken mind. If you have ever had the experience of just knowing what to do in a high-anxiety situation, or had the feeling something was wrong with no concrete proof and found out that you were spot on, then you have experienced it. This is as a result of feeling or listening to your inner voice or…the Real You. We are going to attempt to reveal more of that Real You to you! If you can quiet the analytical mind, with its judgments and opinions, and open up that inner you who doesn't judge, watches with attention, and acts out of compassion, you will have come a step closer to what Eastern religions have called enlightenment, Christians have called Christ consciousness, and Western culture has called serenity.

While we can't extinguish the analytical mind, nor would we want to, we seek to balance our life and harmonize the components of our being. We seek to bring unity to ourselves, our mind, body, and spirit.

If you think you might like to try to put a little bit more of that in your life, then you are ready to take the first step. If you've tried other things and they haven't worked for you, forget them. Jump into the driver's seat and test drive the Real You. I think you're going to like it.

━◄+ +►━

What is Conscious Driving?

You may be thinking that you have never driven "unconsciously." I have.

Have you ever driven somewhere automatically only to find out that you didn't mean to drive there? I have. I was going from home to the mall near my office on the weekend and ended up in the parking lot of my office. I pulled into my usual parking spot at work and then the light bulb went off over my head. *It's Saturday and my office is closed.* I was actually supposed to be going to the mall.

Have you ever driven past your exit because you were lost in thought? I have...a number of times.

Most of us drive on autopilot more than we care to admit. We aren't driving unsafely or unlawfully. We just aren't driving with our full attention on what we are doing. Why? We have a lot of things on our mind. We snap back to attention when something demands it. A deer in the road. Another driver swerving into our lane. An accident up ahead. But we certainly aren't normally fully present as drivers.

There is something about driving a car that is very close to the relationship humans have with breathing. We can do it without thinking or paying close attention to it. But we can bring our attention back to it when we feel it is necessary. The way we drive can be observed just like the way we breathe. When we are scared, we may take a deep, sudden breath inward. When driving, we may slam on the brakes. When we are agitated, we may breathe quickly and shallowly. When driving while agitated, we may speed up, brake quickly, and change lanes often. The way we drive says a lot about our state of mind, just like our observed breathing.

Meditators have for centuries used the breath as a way to calm the mind and slow the thoughts and physical manifestations of emotion. The breath is a gateway between the unconscious mind and the fully conscious mind. When we are not focused on breathing, our unconscious takes over the job. When we focus on the breath, we can control its volume, pace, and character. Thus, the bridge between conscious and unconscious mind.

In meditation, we can use the breath to achieve a clearer, calmer state of mind by employing a clearer, calmer way of breathing.

The same holds true for driving our cars. The connection between unconscious driving and bringing attention to our driving can result in a clearer, calmer way of driving and a clearer, calmer state of being while driving. This clearer, calmer state can then be brought out into the world when you exit your automobile and go on about your daily life.

If you practice this on a regular basis, it can lead to a clearer, calmer life.

How? By allowing you to consciously be in the present moment. By utilizing your time in the car to practice being present in the moment, your mind, body, and spirit learn to work together in unison to allow you to dwell in the now.

What's so great about the now?

Everything. It is the only reality we will ever have. No matter how hard you try to escape the now, you can never do it. Your thoughts can dwell in the past or the future. But you're still in the present. Even ignoring the fact that you are in the present and can only be in the present moment at your present location in the universe, you, in fact, are still forever in the present moment.

The reason that this present moment is so great (besides the fact that it is the only reality there is), is that all things come from the present moment. That means that all creative action and thought comes from the present moment. Everyone and everything in your world only exist and interact at the present moment. It is only at this present moment that you can access the Real You that is behind the delusion of self-concept.

You are not your name, or body, or thoughts. If you change your name, lose a foot, or learn to think in Chinese, are you any less you? If you change your profession, spouse, or location, are you any less the person you really are? No. You are the being that watches all of that happen.

The Real You dwells only in the present moment, in the unmanifested. What does that mean? It means that is the Real You. The you who observes all that is around you and in you. The you who is the watcher of your human experience...is unmanifested, unlimited, and the creative force of this universe. Beyond all concepts, thoughts, and words...you are one with God.

Pretty lofty claim?

Once you experience being in the present moment with no concepts, thoughts, or words, you will be amazed. It cannot be described, only experienced, usually as just a glimpse, at first, but that taste is enough to take you further into your practice. This is the Real You, in the real world, in the present moment only. It has been called satori, enlightenment, or simply being awake! It is not easy. Our human minds have been trained to ignore it, but it is the only real truth we can experience.

It's the feeling of ease without any feeling. It is the clarity of mind with no mind. It is our true nature and it is liberating.

We can learn to focus this attention on the present moment by practicing conscious driving. Many people have practiced it using conscious breathing. You can do this too. You can even do it while driving. In fact, that is a great starting point for you to begin your conscious driving practice.

We can learn to focus our attention on our body, breath, senses, awareness of the road, other drivers, the weather, road conditions, and most of all, our experience in the present moment while driving to bring about a shift in our human experience.

In all of this, we can practice becoming more compassionate as drivers and as human beings.

CHAPTER 3

PAYING ATTENTION

*"In this moment, there is plenty of time. In this moment,
you are precisely as you should be. In this moment,
there is infinite possibility."*

— Victoria Moran

Attention is the ability to focus our awareness on a specific thing…be it an object, experience, thought, sense, or anything else. As easy as that seems to do, it is not easy to hold. Have you ever tried to sit still and pay attention to just one thing for a period of time? It isn't easy. Our natural inclination is to move our attention from one thing to another.

Our thinking has been described as the "monkey mind" because it seems to move constantly, like a monkey moving from tree to tree and to the ground then back into the tree, seemingly never pausing for more than a moment. This never allows us to focus our awareness on anything for more than a superficial moment. We never hold our attention long enough to let the movement subside.

This prevents us from experiencing whatever we are focusing on in any deep and meaningful way. I believe that is why it is so intoxicating to live in a state of monkey mind. Our ego needs to keep our focus off any deep and meaningful awareness to keep itself in control.

As long as we are constantly moving from thought to thought, we will never be able to settle in and realize that we are not our thoughts...we are the one observing our thoughts. Our ego sees that it as a threat to its existence, and immediately tries to stir up feelings, emotions, and thoughts that are strong enough to bring us back into the monkey mind.

Our egoic self finds its origin in the thinking mind. When we assume the belief that the thinking mind is who we are and is the essence of our being, that is when the ego has taken hold of our lives. It becomes stronger over time as we put this egoic identity into practice and feel that we are what we think. The truth is, our thinking mind is simply a tool to be used by us in the physical world to figure out problems, improve our environment, communicate, etc. It is our most valuable tool, but it is not who we are.

Meditation seeks to tame the monkey mind and give us a clearer, calmer look into the real being that is who we really are underneath all of that thinking. It is not easy to do. But with practice, it can become something we can accomplish with a little intention and effort. Once you reach a place of clarity through calming your monkey mind, you will know the peace that is the reward for your efforts. If it didn't provide a sense of better well-being, no one would pursue the practice.

After a while, you find that the calm observer is actually the natural, Real You, and the monkey mind is just an illusion that you thought was you.

So other than sitting in quiet meditation for a period of time, how can we create a practice? By choosing to practice while doing an activity we do every day—driving.

Sure, it's second nature to us. That is why it af
portunity to connect with ourselves on a deep leve
the present moment. The moment that is the only
The moment where the Real You can only exist...the present.

But how does sharpening our ability to hold our attention help? Well, as previously stated, it is the way to slowing down our thoughts and being in the present moment without analyzing, labeling, or judging—just experiencing. If you can notice the space between the thoughts, you have begun to recognize the way to clarity, peace, and experiencing the reality of the now. The only true reality. Here's where it gets tricky—or rather simple but not easy.

If you try to hold onto that space between thoughts, it interrupts the space. If you are trying to hold on but telling yourself not to, that interrupts the space. So how do you hold on without holding on? First, recognize that you are trying to hold onto the space between thoughts. The silence before the next thought. Then breathe, let it go, and bring yourself back to watching that space. You will have to do that over and over and over again. That is what the practice part is. If there are no distractions, it is often easier. Some people find that a little distraction (like white noise) can actually help them stay more focused by offering a consistent distraction that can be tuned out or experienced while observing the space. So they use it as a tool to help them stay focused. The natural road noises, the wind against your car, your tires on the road can serve as your white noise if you like.

With some intentional practice, you can use driving as your practice tool as well. Devoting full attention to driving in the moment, while being totally relaxed, compassionate, and focused, can work as a strong practice. Being distracted by thoughts, noises, or visual stimuli and bringing your focus back to experiencing the present moment (driving your car and breathing) can be your daily practice!

The feel of the wheel, the sound of your tires on the road, the cars passing by, all change constantly in the moment. Experience them and let them go. You can experience the watcher of these senses—the noticer of the experience. This is the Real You underneath all of your thoughts, emotions, and reactions.

Once this is experienced in practice, it will reveal to you the calm, serene, compassionate, joyful being that is the Real You. It may lie under piles of negative thinking, harsh emotions, resentments, and self-criticism, but it is there. It is there in all of us. This is what we intend to evolve into. The real being underneath all of the noise of being human in this day and age. Our egoic thinking minds have cut us off from the timeless, boundless creative force that is the real universe we live in. It has hijacked our natural joyousness and replaced it with judgment, self-doubt, and anxiety.

The process of practice slowly allows us to reveal to ourselves the proper path for our lives. The experience of dwelling in the now allows us to see an unobstructed view of what our life on this earth was truly meant to be and what it can become through the clear experience of reality.

Let me give you an example from my own practice. I can get into the car with a million things on my mind. Problems that exist, problems I'm trying to avoid (real or imagined), projected scenarios where I may be successful, and myriad other thoughts that my thinking, egoic mind would put under the heading of "planning." Although I have very little control over any of the factors that will determine the outcome of any of these situations, my mind will grind away at possible outcomes and ways to manipulate any given situation. The truth is that all of these mental gymnastics will not serve me very well in any way. Most of the energy that goes into these thought processes is totally wasted and will, in fact, never come into play in the real world...which as pointed out earlier, only exists in the now. But this is how my mind has been conditioned to function. I have convinced myself that this way of existence is paramount to my success in the world.

The truth is that all it does is fill me with self-doubt, anxiety, or sometimes a false sense of overconfidence—all of which exist only in my mind. Can my time and energy be better spent on my drive? The answer is yes. How? Seemingly by doing less. By experiencing the Real Me in real time in the current moment. By connecting with the Now.

The first step is to recognize that I have fallen into that old thought pattern that wants to start the thinking process that is only in my mind. Once I recognize I am doing that, I can take steps to bring my attention away from those thoughts and redirect my attention to the current moment. My hands on the steering wheel, the road ahead, the sounds of the road, the feel of the air on my skin. Relaxing my body in the seat and slowing my mind. Once I do this, I notice that there is a little space between the thoughts. They don't go away completely, and I have to keep bringing my attention back away from them and into the present moment. Soon, I notice the calm beginning to wash over me. I notice a sense of clarity entering my mind. I have to keep bringing my attention back into the now, but I notice the flow from racing mind to spacious mind. By the time I get out of the car, all of the thoughts that seemed so important and pressing when I got into the car seem to have faded away, and I walk away a with a calmer and more serene demeanor. It happens to me often, and I am always surprised that it takes me so long to act on my practice when the rewards are so great.

I used to think that I worked things out in my mind while I was driving, and maybe sometimes I really did. But the reality is that most of the time I spent in thought while driving was just my egoic mind exercising its control over my life and creating anxiety while robbing me of experiencing the Real Me in the present moment.

In our practice, we are going to develop a new way of experiencing our reality. We are going to first set our intention to practice, then relax our physical body. Once our intention is set and our body is in a relaxed state, we are going to bring our attention into the present moment with complete awareness, and then work to make that attention as dynamic as the present moment. We are going to use our experience of driving as our dynamic environment to practice in because it is so accessible and second nature to us.

We will learn to use the acronym PRND to remind us of the nature of our practice and help keep us on course. We are used to seeing those letters on the dashboard or console of our car, representing the gear positions of our vehicle—park, reverse, neutral, and drive. We will learn to use these letters to remind us to **P**ractice (intention), **R**elax (bring our awareness into the) **N**ow, and **D**rive (experiencing the dynamic present moment.)

Remember, this moment is the only reality there is. No matter how hard you try, you cannot escape the present moment. This is it! This is reality, and it is here and now whether you choose to experience it directly or not. If you do, you will be amazed at what is revealed. It can allow you to hop into the driver's seat of your life and be aware of your trip down the road of the present moment.

Let's get started!

CHAPTER 4

FIRST THINGS FIRST: INTENTION

*"Let go of your mind and then be mindful.
Close your ears and listen!"*

— Rumi

I ntention can be everything...sometimes. Although the best of intentions can bring about unintended consequences and outcomes, it is a great place to start. If we intend to do good for ourselves, we most often do. Not all the time, of course. We are human. But more often than not, we can see things going sideways and get out of our own way if we choose to. So with that said, let's be sure our intentions are in the right place before we open the door and sit down in the driver's seat.

Let's be sure that our intention is to practice our practice. Which is to say that as we approach our vehicle, we are mindful that we are approaching an opportunity to deepen our practice of mindful, compassionate driving, and that we try to keep this in mind not only when we start the engine, but that we keep reminding ourselves of our intention when we notice our attention drifting.

We have to be careful while doing this. We cannot "pull" ourselves back to attention. We have to recognize what has captured our attention and gently and mindfully return that attention to our practice. Otherwise, our attention is more focused on the interruption (be it an inward thought or outward distraction), thus making it stronger. For example, I am driving down the interstate and am aware of the feeling of my hands on the wheel, my car passing the guardrails, and the sound of the air as my car passes through it at 55 miles per hour. I drift off into thought and notice that I am thinking about picking up coffee on the way home after work. Once I notice myself getting off track (out of the present moment), I can acknowledge the fact that I am thinking about buying coffee and refocus my attention to my breathing in and out as I drive (a technique you may become very familiar with once you find how well it works).

If I say to myself, "Oh no...I've stopped practicing awareness of the present moment and am thinking about coffee. How did that happen? I can't do that anymore. In fact, don't think about coffee...wait...don't think about not thinking about coffee...wait..." You can see where this is going. If I do that, I am continuing, and in fact strengthening, the process of getting off track. That is my cue to pause for a second and think of nothing, then bring my attention back to my breathing or whatever it was my intention to be aware of. The point is, don't panic. It will happen. A lot! That is really why the practice exists. If you could just jump in your car and be totally aware in the present moment and not be distracted by thoughts of past or future, you wouldn't need a practice.

The point is to grow through the experience of getting sidetracked and redirecting your attention. You will find it is not easy to stay on point. This will allow you to recognize how deeply entrenched in our life process the control of our distracted monkey mind is.

So intend to practice, but not to be perfect. There is nothing to really achieve. It is an experience, just like all of life. What it does do for you is allow you to develop a deeper experience over time as you continue to practice. The Real You emerges in a new, fresh manner that will reward you in the most subtle and life changing ways.

So it is important not to fight distraction but to embrace it as a transformative practice tool. You can learn to transcend the distraction—that is what is important. The more you experience it and transcend or transform it, the easier it is to recognize that this process can take place both in and out of the car. You will notice it at work, at home, it will pop into your field of awareness here and there at first. As you practice, it will become second nature, and hopefully, with diligent and meaningful practice, work its way into your mode of being.

Carry this intention as you enter your car, and keep it in mind as your drive. Which brings me to my second intention. It is also important for your intention to be keeping your attention in the moment as you exit the vehicle and step forth into the world.

Some people keep little reminders on their desk, refrigerator, or bathroom mirror to keep their focus on their practice. Your practice can become your way of being...after all, there is no dress rehearsal for life. This is it. It is vitally important not to miss it!

Please think of your practice not as something you are trying to do. Rather, think of it as something you are being. I am being present in this moment. I am experiencing myself directly in this exact moment by being here in full awareness of the reality of now. There really is no other reality to experience.

If you have never practiced this type of thing before, it may sound like a lot of esoteric bull. I urge you to give it a try anyway.

Be open minded and really set your intention as you unlock your car door and sit in the driver's seat. You have nothing to lose by trying. Often, people don't really understand the concepts and language of the teachings of practice until they have had some experience with which to relate to it.

Many times, it is only a brief, fleeting moment of awareness. It disappears as soon as we recognize it and start consciously thinking about how we are experiencing it. It is the space between thoughts. The pause at the end of a breath. The silent anticipation of sound. If you can catch a glimpse, you can get a sense of the experience of the now. That is what keeps us coming back to practice!

Be sure to keep your intention as simply that, an intention. It is not a steadfast goal that you seek to accomplish. There is no end game. By intending to practice and renewing our intention when we get distracted, we nurture our path into the now. Getting knocked off the path and getting reset is one of the best trans-formative exercises in our practice. It is important to learn that when we get knocked down, we must get up. Otherwise, we will never know the transformation that present moment awareness can bring to our lives.

I have had some driving experiences that seemed to be a con-stant cycle of setting my intention to practice, getting distracted, and resetting my intention again, only to get distracted once more. These experiences can be frustrating, but ultimately, they are a true test of our dedication to practice diligently. If it was easy, there would be no effort involved. True change requires that old ways are confronted and new ways are skillfully introduced. We need to experience this change at a basic organic level over time. Since we are not learning a new way of being so much as we are, over time, *experiencing* a new way of being, it is going to require repetition, examination, and adjustment. Do not be discouraged.

When you reset your intention to practice, do so with all of your being. Truly clear any frustration or bodily tension and begin anew. Just as each moment is a completely new moment in your experience of the present, let every reset of your intention to practice be a new start, free of any distraction from the previous moment. Intention is about trusting the process and expecting to encounter obstacles. It is important to be open to that process and trust that your intention to renew your intention when you are knocked off your path is available and effective. This "intention to renew your intention" can give you a sense of power over any distractions that may hijack your focus on awareness of the present moment. Know that by bringing your attention back to renewing intention, you can remove the energy from the distraction and dissolve its power.

Your intention can give you the power to practice effectively in any given situation. How? You are telling yourself, "I am going to do it!" How are you going to do it? By doing it. It is that simple. That is how it works. No fear. No self-doubt. Those are manufactured by the mind. Intention has no room for anything other than doing what is intended. Keep it that simple.

Your intention will keep you connected to the now, and your practice can flow from moment to moment, unimpeded by distractions. As you experience the integration of intention in your practice over time, it will become second nature, and distractions will diminish. Part of the process is that over time, distractions, in general, lose their power over your present moment awareness as you recognize them as only distractions to be handled and not as impediments to your practice. They are in fact an integral part of your practice.

With your experiences in practice of how intention is effective in aligning you with the truth of the present moment, you will begin to notice that you are using it more and more in your daily life outside of your practice. You can use intention to learn how to effectively deal with your fear, anxiety, and self-doubt. Intention can be a clean-cutting laser to the truth—the truth that the only thing holding you back from doing what you really want to do is you. It is not enough to be told that you can overcome your fears and self-doubt; it must be experienced. This is where the true benefits of experiencing the results of intention in your practice can transform your life outside of your vehicle.

It is worth keeping in mind that you alone are responsible for your intention and the care and feeding of that intention. No one is going to be behind you urging you on or checking on you to make you sure you are doing what you intended to do. It is easy to give up when problems make your practice require diligent effort. It is at those times that the biggest lessons are revealed and the most is learned. Often, when one starts out on a path of self-discovery using a set of techniques or a program to help them and it doesn't work for them, they blame the program. It was too weird, too rigid, too time-consuming, or just didn't make sense once they got into it. This may be the case for some, but for others, it is just that they didn't want it. If it came easily, they would have been fine. But once it required leaving their comfort zone, they became uncomfortable and quit. This program requires that you leave your comfort zone. It takes dedicated, repeated, intention and will no doubt not be the easy way out. Anything worth doing to make a profound change in your life seldom is.

How many times have you heard of someone going into something with the best of intentions, only to have things not work out and they give up? It happens all the time. Maybe part of the problem is that they go into it with the best of intentions, but they don't renew their intention when they get knocked off course or distracted along the way. This is one of the most valuable tools you can develop through your driving practice—perseverance!

When you go through a whole commute in your car and never really seem to settle into current moment awareness, when you have dealt with distractions that didn't seem to dissolve at all, or when you feel your practice is stuck and maybe this is as far as it can take you, persevere! Take a break. Put on some music for a little bit. Get your mind off of your practice and settle back into your comfort zone. Once you feel distracted enough that you are comfortable again, reset your intention to practice and get back at it. You'll be surprised at how refreshing it can be to again follow your intended path.

Intention is the gate through which we enter our practice. It is a gateless gate that must be conceived of in the thinking mind and then forgotten as the intention is brought into practice. It must be called upon again and again to set us back on the right path. Experience the power of intention, and it will transform the way you think, act, and live.

CHAPTER 5

RELAX

*"The paradox of relaxation is the renewal of mind;
rekindle of spirit and revitalize of strength."*

— Lailah Gifty Akita

Relaxation is one of the key components of living a centered, conscious existence. Most of us need to learn to relax. It doesn't come naturally. Relaxation is not only a part of our driving practice, it is a practice unto itself. The more you practice conscious relaxation, the more you will find it easier to access your conscious relaxation when you need it.

Being in a relaxed state not only makes us calmer and more serene, it actually changes the way our body functions. Our heart rate slows, as does our breathing and blood pressure. Our muscles relax and our digestion becomes comfortable. Our mind stops racing and slows to a comfortable rhythm. This is where we need to be to embark on being in the now. Stress and anxiety are the distractions that make solid practice difficult. By reducing or eliminating these distractions, we can see clearly into the now. It is like the muddied waters of a pond, where all we see is the surface of the dark water. Once the agitation stops, the water calms and the sediment falls to the bottom. Only then can we see "into" the water and realize its true depth.

Have you ever heard of someone going out to take a relaxing drive? Yeah, so have I. Who is this person who finds driving relaxing? Sure, if you're driving along one of those deserted country roads with no other cars on them on a beautiful, picturesque day, like in the car commercials in a luxury sports car or sedan, it might be relaxing. But in reality, you are driving in the car you can afford along a busy street with a hundred other drivers, all trying to get to where they are going in the least amount of time. No doubt your mind and theirs are going in a million different directions while you navigate through traffic, just wanting to get there.

One of the chief caveats of centering yourself for the practice of mindfulness or any meditation is to relax your body. It is impossible to relax your mind if your body is not in some way relaxed. Everyone can have a different idea of what it means to relax. Some people relax with an invigorating run or bike ride, others with an interesting book or TV show. That is not what I am referring to. I am talking about physically relaxing your muscles and connective tissues. Your limbs and bones. Your inner physical body and energy. This is something you will have to keep an eye on as you practice. I find myself checking back on it multiple times every few minutes.

When you first approach your vehicle, take a deep breath and try to relax your shoulders and neck. Sit in the seat and be aware of the feeling of your body in the contours of the seat. Notice your breathing. Take note of the rise and fall of your torso as you breathe, and consciously try to breathe deep into your abdomen. Try to make your breaths long and relaxed. Watching the breath is one of the best ways to relax the mind and body.

Your breathing obviously happens unconsciously as you go throughout your waking day and, of course, as you sleep. Your body and brain keep your breath rhythmically moving to keep you oxygenated and alive. All of this usually happens outside of your conscious awareness. If you ever take the time to notice your breathing, it is then brought within the awareness of your consciousness. As you move away from that awareness, your unconscious mind takes over the operation again.

This is what makes the breath such a great gateway to conscious attention. It is always there, and awareness of it can move back and forth between the conscious and unconscious awareness of your mind. That is why it is such a great tool for calming your body. When your mind is upset or in a state of anxiousness, your breathing becomes rapid and shallow. When you are relaxed and at ease, your breathing is deep and slow. Using these breathing patterns as cues for your body, we can slow the breath and our body reacts by relaxing.

So keep an eye on your breathing. Check it periodically, and be sure to slow it down when necessary.

Another aspect of relaxing behind the wheel is to scan your body for tension. I personally tend to tense up in my shoulders and neck when I drive. I notice this tension almost every time I remember to consciously check my body. Then I drop my shoulders and relax the muscles in my neck while I take a deep relaxing breath. I need to do this repeatedly. I also check my legs, arms, hands, and back, scanning and relaxing as needed to keep myself physically loose and tension free. A periodic check of your body can head off any building of tension in your muscles. This can be accomplished through progressive muscle relaxation—tensing and relaxing individual muscle groups and feeling the relaxation wash over them. I start with my legs and work my way up my body. I keep my awareness on my driving and my body, especially as it relates to my comfort in the car. Often, I notice that the way I have my hands on the steering wheel creates undue tension in my shoulders. I adjust my grip or the position of my arm to a more relaxed posture. I adjust my feet and legs for maximum relaxation of my lower extremities, all while paying present moment awareness to my driving and my body as it controls the vehicle.

The object is not to become a flaccid bag of muscles in your skin, but rather to relax your body enough so that it does not become a distraction to your practice and will allow you to feel comfortable in the present moment. Be sure to check and recheck your body several times throughout your practice. You will begin to notice where your persistent trouble areas are, and from that, you can more easily make the adjustments necessary to make yourself comfortable in your seat and in your practice. You might even enjoy your conscious relaxation and bring it out into other experiences in your life. Sitting at your desk, watching television, reading, or even just walking.

This practice is also good for bringing conscious awareness to your body in the present moment. If ever there was a way to bring you into the now, it is through your body. Your body is your connection to the here and now in this world. Being in the now and feeling your body with complete awareness in this space at this time is your reality in this world. In this way, consciously relaxing your body and breath is your practice.

Be sure to practice this even when you are not driving. At home on the couch, in bed at night, in a restaurant, or at work, the benefits of conscious relaxation are numerous and always readily accessible. Just be sure to make it part of your practice, and it will become part of your everyday living.

Conscious relaxation has many benefits besides making us feel more at ease. It improves our ability to focus our attention. This is of great value when developing our awareness of the present moment...especially while driving. It reduces the activity of stress hormones, improves blood flow, and lowers fatigue. All of these can add to the distractions that we will face in our practice. It certainly helps if we can eliminate or minimize these distractions through relaxation.

Stress can bring about tension, and tension can bring about stress. They feed off of each other and can lead to anxiety and a weakened, tired mind. If we can step in consciously and relieve the tension in our bodies, we can break this cycle. Stress will be reduced, which will reduce tension. Now the cycle is working for the betterment of ourselves and our practice...and all because we put forth a little intention and effort.

The type of relaxation we are talking about is mostly a physical relaxing of the body. We are not referring to deeper forms of relaxation techniques such as autogenic training or any type of deep meditative relaxation. These are fine for time spent sitting quietly by yourself, but not for a driving practice. The type of physical relaxation we are proposing should relieve you of any physical tension, make you relaxed but energized, and is more intended to remove any discomfort that might distract you from your current moment awareness of the road and your experience of driving in the now.

Since you will be moving while driving, navigating with the steering wheel, foot on the accelerator and brake, and moving your head to see the road and mirrors, this type of relaxation is more akin to a moving relaxation. Not as dynamic as walking or yoga, but feeling a calm relaxation while moving the necessary parts of your body to drive. The aim is more to relieve the tension that is brought about by egoic states of mind, emotional and mental tension, and just plain old bodily tension due to the pressures of living on a schedule.

The very act of present moment awareness will also diminish stress and tension on its own. It is in this way that a conscious relaxation of one's body, coupled with your experience in the now, can build off of each other to maintain your relaxed and open body and mind. By rechecking your body and keeping it relaxed, you will notice that it will become easier and easier as you progress in your practice. When you employ the techniques you have used in your driving practice outside the car, you will find they work just as well to keep you serene and relaxed in any environment.

As your body relaxes, so will your mind. The body is a great gateway to the mind, and vice versa. It is the union of mind and body that help produce a calm demeanor when entering into your practice. As you draw your mental attention into your body, you are moving your attention into the now without even realizing it. As you scan and feel your body, you are witnessing the physical feelings of your joints and muscles in the now. Relax your mind with your body and you will be in a better state to begin your journey into the now.

As you learn to savor the current moment awareness you experience while in your driving practice, you will also notice that you are cultivating a sense of gratitude. This springs forth from a relaxed "knowing" that you are in the right place. Where else could you possibly be? This state of relaxed knowing leads to a sense of oneness with where you are and what you are doing. That is to say that you are in union with the now. You are in union with the Truth. You are the Truth. The thing is, you have always been and will always be the Truth. It is when we experience this directly and know it beyond words or thought that we sense who we really are. Some of us may feel this for the first time, and it will be a profound experience. It is described as a spiritual experience by some. The Zen Buddhists call it satori, which means "seeing into one's true nature." I just like to call it the Truth.

This may seem like a lot to absorb before taking your first steps in a driving practice, but it is important to know that being in a relaxed state is necessary for you to hold present moment awareness for any amount of time. Even if you have a drive where you don't ever clear away all of the distraction, at least you will be physically relaxed and better able to act in a serene way when you get out of your car. So we have set our intention and have a relaxed mind and body. It is time to turn the key in the ignition and take the next step into our practice. Although it is not going to be a bumpy ride, it is important to put your seat belt on. Be sure to practice safe driving techniques at all times when developing your driving practice. The rewards are many.

CHAPTER 6

BEING IN THE NOW

*"Few of us ever live in the present. We are forever
anticipating what is to come or remembering
what has gone."*

— Louis L'Amour

Now is the only reality we have. Everything else is just our mind creating a future that doesn't yet exist or remembering a past that no longer exists. No matter how hard we try, we can never truly escape the now. When people talk about stopping to smell the flowers, they are talking about taking the time to stop our minds and be fully present in the now. This is the only way to experience the true joy of living. We may have fond memories or happy future expectations to look forward to, but ultimately, they are not real. The feelings we experience as a result of these memories or projections might feel real in the now, but they are not based in reality. They are our mind's formulation only and do not really exist. They are like movies playing in our minds that

41

bring us some enjoyment, but also sadness, anxiety, and anger. Ultimately, they are not real and are not us. They are merely concepts our mind and ego have created that take us away from the real joy we could be experiencing in the present moment.

There are myriad books, recordings, articles, and videos from some very wise and experienced people who can tell you a lot about the now...the present moment. If you don't grasp the concept of what is so special about being in total awareness of the present moment, I encourage you to seek out their stories, concepts, and ideas. Although it is a very simple concept, it is not always easy to understand, or grasp why it is important. Some have suggested that learning to dwell in the present is the next evolutionary stage of humankind. I tend to agree with them.

Every emotion the mind conjures up either through thought, our mind's interpretation of an experience, or our perceptions of others, is filtered through our ego and past experiences. Remembering the past is how we learn, but that only goes so far. Learning from our mistakes helps us to avoid the same mistake in the future. But filtering all experiences through the mind obscures the direct connection with the reality that is the present moment. Our thinking is a marvelous thing, but it is severely limited and limiting. It is tainted by emotion, our sense of separateness from the world and others around us, and all of the thought that is based on drastically limited experience.

If we can remove the screen of our thinking, egoic mind, we can experience life as it is—unfiltered and pure. This is the miracle of direct experience. It makes the ordinary magical and carries with it the freedom of limitless acceptance and ultimately, true joy. Words can refer or point to it, but it can only be found through direct experience. You can seek out the signs pointing the way, but only by walking the path yourself can you reach the fullness of direct experience.

The Dalai Lama points out that people are so anxious about the future that they do not enjoy the present; the result being that they do not live in the present or the future. Since you can't live in the future, and you are focused on it with all your attention, you miss the present moment that actually does exist. In that way, you miss it all. You are left with only your egoic mind and a false reality that leads to dissatisfaction and unhappiness. The way out of this mindset is to bring your attention back to the truth—the experience of the present moment reality—with all of your awareness.

And so it is in practicing to experience this reality directly that we can find our way to it. So set your intention to practice; relax your body, breathing, and mind. Then bring your focused attention to the now.

For me, usually, when I focus my attention in the now in my driving practice, the first thing I notice is my visual space. I see through the windshield of the car the horizon, trees, buildings, and the road. I notice that my peripheral vision comes into my field of attention. Then I feel my hands on the wheel, my legs on the seat, even the feel of my clothes on my skin and the rising and falling of my torso as I breathe. The air going in and out of my nostrils, the temperature of the air, and the sound of the engine. I see my hands on the wheel, the interior of the vehicle, and my movement as the car is in motion.

I feel the bumps and unevenness in the road, and sometimes its smoothness. I keep my awareness focused on my direct experience of everything around me with every sense I have. My mind is free of thought and riding the wave of being in the now. It is hard at first to not slide back into thinking "Wow! This is amazing!" But then you have slipped back into the thinking mind and have started analyzing the experience through the filter of the mind and emotions. Time to get back on track. Take a breath, relax, and bring your attention back to the present moment.

One thing I kept doing when I first started to develop this practice was to mentally list everything I saw. Road sign, tractor trailer, speed limit 65 sign…this was not good. Being present and experiencing the moment isn't about bringing the experience into a narrated thought list. It is difficult to avoid doing this at first because our minds are untrained. We are used to putting any experience through the lens of our egoic mind in order to accept it as a real experience. Nothing could be further from the truth. In thinking about what we are experiencing, we are taking away from the experiencing of the moment by putting attention on what our mind thinks or sees in the experience instead of the pure experience itself.

When this happens, try to relax and start again. Just be in the moment. Notice, but do not mentally comment or list things in a mental conversation in your mind. Try to keep your thinking mind silent by focusing more attention on the experiencing. At first, this will come in very small increments. Do not be discouraged. It is akin to the silence between notes in music, or the pause between inhalation and exhalation.

Reality is dynamic and always advancing. Our minds try to stop that advancing dynamic so as to have power over it. The problem is that we cannot have power over something that no longer exists.

As an example, if I am driving and notice a deer in a field next to the highway, my mind might say "Oh look a deer!" So I have had the experience of noticing and being aware of the deer standing in the field as I travel down the road. Then I think, "That was pretty cool. I don't see many deer anymore. Seems like I used to see a lot more when I was a kid. Maybe I just noticed them more because I was looking out the side window of the back seat instead of driving back then...wait! What am I doing? I've just spent fifteen seconds of my drive in my own mind rather than in reality."

So my mind managed to stop my awareness of reality for fifteen seconds, just like that.

And with that, it hijacks my attention and takes it away from the reality of the present moment. My thinking, egoic mind usually hijacked my entire trip when I drove before beginning a practice. That's why I could drive by my exit or not be aware of anything around me as I drove. I put my driving on autopilot and let my thinking mind steal my reality...or rather, steal me away *from* reality.

Upon beginning my practice, I noticed that I was lucky if I could get my mind to stop long enough to get fifteen seconds of pure awareness in the moment. In fact, the first time I was able to do that, I found it to be simply amazing! It was from these small increments of clear awareness that I was able to build my practice and have the motivation to practice every time I sat down in the driver's seat and even elsewhere.

When you are starting a practice, this will happen more often than not. What I mean to say is that you will spend more time as the thinking, egoic mind than you will as the experiencer of the now. This is to be expected. You have been programmed from birth to use your thinking mind like this, which is why you feel that you are your mind, your thoughts, and your feelings. This is not the truth. You are the observer of your mind, your thoughts, and your feelings.

Our conditioning has led us to the point in human evolution where we are built for success but programmed for failure. Again, do not be discouraged! There has not been anyone who has been able to maintain a perfect 24/7 practice in life. After all, we are human and at a point in history where we are just beginning to realize our situation and perhaps taking the first steps to true freedom in reality.

What I have found to be effective in this battle against the strength of the egoic mind is to simply surrender. Surrender to win. This may be the most important weapon in our arsenal for positive change. If we try to push back against our own mind, we only strengthen it. The key is to become pliable and yielding to its force, thus rendering it ineffective. Through acceptance and surrender, we transcend the egoic mind.

As an example, let's say I am driving and see a deer by the side of the road, and then the egoic mind takes over and I begin thinking about the deer, drifting off of the awareness of the present moment. I can pause, accept that the egoic mind has taken over, reset my intention, relax, and bring my attention back to the reality of the present moment. Conversely, if I think "Ugghhhh...I did it again. Why can't I stop doing that? Get out of my mind... mind!" I am not only remaining in the egoic mind and away from reality, I am strengthening my ego by pushing back against it with more thought. The egoic mind doesn't care if you are mad at it or hate it, as long as you recognize its existence as your reality. It could go on forever like that, making you uncomfortable with anxiety, taking all of your energy away from the present reality, becoming a bigger and stronger part of who you think you are.

It is important to not feel as though your egoic mind is someone else living inside your head. It is simply your mind getting stuck in its own thought patterns...its own reality. You can see that your higher self is the one who notices your egoic mind and its racing, erratic ways. So surrender to the fact that it is a part of you. Don't let the fact that it drives you crazy actually drive you crazy! Accept it as a great gift that just needs to be worked on and recognized for what it is...your intelligence on a thinking level (which is different from your intelligence on an experiential level of reality, or spiritual intelligence). As soon as you are not pushing back against your egoic mind or feeding it with more and more focus and attention, it will collapse in on itself.

So proceed with a sense of freedom and experimentation. Practice is not a means to an end. Some musicians or athletes may practice in anticipation of a performance or a big game. When we endeavor to clear our minds so that we are completely aware in the present moment, the practice *is* our performance. The only big game is the one that is going on at this very moment in perpetuity. The only reality there will ever be is the one that is happening right now, and you don't want to miss it!

CHAPTER 7

DRIVE

"It isn't by getting out of the world that we become enlightened, but by getting into the world...by getting so tuned in that we can ride the waves of our existence and never get tossed because we become the waves."

— Ken Kesey,

Reality is forever dynamic. Our minds try to freeze time with memories or jump ahead in time with projection. We daydream a false reality that never really exists. In this way, we miss the real life we are living.

Driving is also dynamic. We are moving, stopping, starting, parking, etc. We are going from point A to point B and everywhere in between. But we can only do this one millisecond at a time through the present moment in reality. If we match our attention with our driving, with both being in the present moment of reality, great things happen. We become a more attentive, compassionate, cooperative, and safer driver. We can eliminate the distractions

that daydreaming, mind-created emotional thinking, and projecting into the future can cause.

We can pay attention to the road, our speed, our relationship
to other vehicles, and our surroundings. We get a deeper feeling
for our hands on the wheel, our foot on the gas or brake pedal,
and we notice more about our entire driving experience with all
of our senses. Attempting to eliminate distracted driving from our
life can be a very positive change to the way some of us drive.

When first beginning my practice, I had to eliminate as many
distractions as possible to make it easier for myself to relax and
focus my attention on the now. I turned off the music, silenced
my phone, and didn't bring drinks or food with me. I could just
drive and focus on what I was doing, seeing, and experiencing. I
remember having to take an hour and a half drive to see a client
when I first started practicing. I looked at it as both an opportunity
to really challenge my practice and a challenge to not use all of
my usual devices to fight the boredom of the long drive. Usually, I
had an extra-large coffee next to me, the music blasting, my phone
on the console face up, and a few snacks on my passenger's seat.
In other words, I was doing everything possible to drive without
experiencing the drive.

I silenced the self-doubt in my mind by starting the practice
right out of the driveway. After a few fits and starts, bringing my
attention back to the moment only to lose it quickly, I noticed that
I was putting more and more space between those slips back into
my thinking. By the end of the first half hour, it was getting pretty smooth. I also noticed that when I did slip back into my egoic
thinking mind, I was not so disturbed by the fact that it happened.
I would just effortlessly bring my attention back into the now. Not
only was I able to experience more of the now, I was able to experience a nonjudgmental transition back from the egoic mind
into the now. That was a great gift in itself. I wasn't sweating the

inevitability that I was going to slip back into my thoughts. This contributed greatly to a more relaxed and rewarding experience.

By the end of my long drive, I reached my client's office in a very clear and relaxed state. I tried to duplicate that experience on my trip back. Interestingly, I was not able to. Driving and reality are both dynamic, and as such, experiences can only be similar but never duplicated. I had a great trip back, but it was different. Maybe a little less of a revelation and more of a relaxed practice. Nevertheless, quite a bit different from my previous distracted driving experiences on the same trip before I developed a practice.

I noticed a lot more about my environment than I ever had before as well. I started to notice the exit numbers that corresponded to the towns. I noticed the snow on the tops of the hills that lingered when the lower elevations were snow free. I heard the tires on the road, felt the bottoms of my feet in my shoes, and noticed that my speed was much closer to the posted speed limit than it had been on prior trips. All in all, it was a much more mindful experience, and I felt more relaxed than I had on any other trip to this client's office.

Once I had built up a pretty regular practice and was noticing the subtle changes in myself as I drove, I began to occasionally bring along a coffee. I incorporated the sense of taste into my driving practice as I sipped the coffee. I didn't drink it absentmindedly. I felt the rim of the plastic top on my lips, the heat of the liquid, the taste of the beverage on my tongue, and the feel of it as I swallowed. I brought mindfulness into the experience of driving while drinking a cup of coffee. It is important to keep attention on the actual driving at all times. If you notice that your focus is very deep into the experience of drinking the beverage at the expense of your attention on driving your vehicle, then perhaps you should experience the drinking of the beverage before or after driving. Trying to bounce to another experience is a very subtle thing and must be done with the utmost of care to avoid distraction. Remember, our main focus is to practice awareness of the now while driving. You are going to discover the subtleties of being fully aware of more than one task at a time as your practice progresses.

To be sure, it is the point of learning this practice so we can bring it into other aspects of our life. But just as the meditation practitioner develops his or her practice "on the cushion" and brings that experience into other "outside" experiences, it is our aim to develop our practice initially while driving.

The same holds true for music. I started with instrumental music only. I could notice it in the background of my experience without being distracted from my driving experience, and without my mind identifying with the songs. I took this in baby steps and would often have to turn it off if I noticed the least bit of distraction developing. In no way would I recommend talk radio or news. These can really take over your attention and are, in fact, a purposeful distraction for most people.

In a previous chapter, I wrote about the epidemic of road rage and how destructive it is to our driving, our fellow humans, and our peace. This is largely due to an extreme lack of patience. Patience with our own schedules, other drivers, our lives in general, and most of all ourselves. The very definition of patience is the capacity to accept or tolerate delay, trouble, or suffering without getting angry or upset. Often, when we encounter these on the road, we feel the need to react without outrage and indignation. We feel we have a right to respond strongly and are justified in doing so. That is pure ego at work.

Practicing patience goes against our egoic instincts. However, through our practice, patience can be learned and integrated into our behavior. It usually isn't something that comes naturally to most of us. But people who are able to practice patience have an easier time in their driving practice as well as out in the world.

If we can cultivate patience in our practice, we will gain a valuable tool in our life outside of our practice. We will learn to be able to relax in the face of incidents on the road that may otherwise have resulted in thoughts of road rage or some form of unrest in ourselves. We will be able to better recognize a lack of patience in others and better understand their reactions. We will hopefully be more patient out in the world, especially with ourselves, and foster better relationships and outcomes in our dealings with other people.

When you practice patience you are practicing peace. Serenity will grow in your life, and you will wonder why you ever let yourself get so upset over things that were ultimately out of your control anyway. We are used to wanting things to happen immediately and just the way we would like them to. This is seldom realistic. If we can live in the now, we can adjust ourselves to recognize that the flow of life has its own time and its own agenda. It is up to us to do our best to change what we can for ourselves, but also learn to accept life on life's terms. That will bring us harmony and union with the reality of the present moment and, ultimately, a more peaceful and fulfilling life.

I had an incident once where this really played out. I had ordered an appliance from our local home center and it was to be delivered and installed on a certain day, at a certain time. Things got screwed up, and the item was brought for delivery with no installation person. It was a clothes dryer that needed to be carried down into the basement, installed, and the old dryer removed. It had already been on order for a week, so there were heaps of my family's unwashed clothing piled up that needed washing and drying. The delivery person told my wife that he could only drop it off in the garage. My wife called me at my office, and my first reaction was anger. I told my wife to refuse delivery and under no circumstances was she to sign off on any delivery without installation and removal of the old dryer.

On my way home from work, I intended to stop in at the home center and straighten those people out. I was ready for a confrontation. As I walked to my car, a thought flashed through my mind. Maybe anger and confrontation would not be the best route. As I sat behind the wheel, I set my intention to practice mindful driving on the way to the store to at least calm myself down before the confrontation. I relaxed and brought my attention away from the anger in my mind and into the now. I put the car in drive and headed out for the home center. I had to keep reminding myself to be patient. Flashes of anger and projection about the confrontation I was going to have with the employees at the store kept derailing my attention, but I was persistent and patient in my practice.

By the time I arrived, I felt much calmer and clearheaded. That burning feeling of anger had subsided, and I realized I was only there to solve a problem. I thought to myself, *What is the best way to solve a problem involving people who don't know you?* The answer came immediately. *Be patient and ask them for help in solving your problem.* My egoic thinking immediately rose up and conjured thoughts of needing to have an angry confrontation in order to get what I rightly paid for. I was centered enough through my experience on the drive there to make the decision to give a calm and patient approach a try first. I told myself that if I got nowhere being patient, I always had the option of letting my ego take the driver's seat, although my experience has been that people seldom respond to an irate, angry customer anymore.

I set my intention to be patient. I took a deep breath and relaxed my body. I walked into the store and stepped up to the customer service desk, where I introduced myself politely, explained what had happened, and asked if there was anyone there who could help me. Soon, I had the appliance manager, the customer service representative, and an employee from the lumber department trying to help me. In the end, the manager decided to take the company's rental truck, load the dryer himself, and drive it to my house right then. He told me he didn't have any experience hooking up a dryer, but at least it would be in my basement, and he could take the old one back with him. Then, another store employee who was at the desk chimed in and said that he had hooked up plenty of dryers and that if I already had the electrical outlet in place, it would be no problem. The manager asked him if he would mind leaving his department to help me out. He smiled and said it would be a pleasure.

In the end, I had my dryer installed that night, the old one taken away, more apologies than I can mention from the manager, and an extra discount for my trouble. I doubt I would have gotten the same results if I had gone in confrontational and angry. I'm not saying that patience and kindness always get you exactly what you want, but it sure is a great place to start. I will always be sure to focus my attention on developing patience in my driving practice and in my life…I hope you can, too.

Make driving your refuge, the time when you can experience the now in relative peace. You'll begin to notice that you start to look forward to the time you spend behind the wheel. Develop your practice, and it will develop your life into a more serene, patient, and compassionate experience.

CHAPTER 8

PRND

"Through recognizing and realizing the empty essence,
instead of being selfish and self-centered, one feels very
open and free"

— Tsoknyi Rinpoche

When I first started developing my driving practice, I noticed that as soon as I sat in the driver's seat, right in front of my face was a great tool to remind me of my practice and the important keys to staying on track. It is PRND. This usually stands for park, reverse, neutral, and drive and is found on your dashboard, steering column, or perhaps on your center console gearshift. I use it to remind myself of the some of the keys to action in my practice and refer to it several times a trip...sometimes more! Here is my breakdown:

P is for PRACTICE
When I first sit in the driver's seat, I make it a point to look at the PRND on my dash. I focus on P for a moment and move my

attention to awareness of my intention to practice mindful driving. In this way, I "set" my intention for the trip. I know from experience that I will have to "reset" this intention several times, if not more, during my drive.

If I get off track and need to reset my intention, it helps me to remember that I am practicing driving. I reset my intention to practice my awareness of the present moment...reality. When my attention drifts and I notice that I am thinking thoughts of the past, future, or anything but focusing my attention on the present moment, I refer to my dashboard and think *P...Practice*. This helps give me the ability to break the mental thought stream that was not in the present moment. I reset.

R is for RELAX

After my intention is mentally set, I then move on to the next reminder on the dash, R for Relax. I scan my body for any tension points and consciously release them. I take a deep breath and rescan until I am pretty sure I am as relaxed as I can get at the moment.

Whenever I notice that I am drifting off of the present moment (i.e., in where my thoughts and attention are focused) and do a reset, I also usually notice that I have built up tension somewhere in my body. For me, it is most often in my shoulders. I take a quick scan of my body and note any areas of tension. Then I make a conscious effort to relax and let the tension dissolve. This may involve taking another deep breath and letting it flow out of me as I refocus my attention on the present moment. It will all become fluid after some practice.

N is for NOW

Once I have focused my intention and relaxed my body, I bring my attention into the now. I observe my surroundings visually without mentally narrating what I see. I feel my hands on the wheel, I hear the starting of the engine as I feel the turn of the key. I smell the air and feel its temperature on my nostrils. I do all of this while remaining relaxed and keeping my focus on the unfolding moment.

If I notice that my mind is starting to comment, narrate, or drift into any thought, I bring my attention back to the present moment—my breathing, my surroundings, the feelings in my body or on my skin. I feel myself sitting in the seat. Then I reset, practice, relax, now.

D is for Drive

Everything we have done to this point has been leading up to this moment. The moment when we put the car and our practice into drive. As your vehicle moves through space in the present moment, so do you. This is your time to focus all of your attention on the experience of driving and awareness of all the sights, sounds, tactile sensations, smells, movements, stillness, and freedom of driving in the now.

Your intention has been set to practice, you are relaxed, you have turned your attention to the now, your mind is not encumbered by thought. You have the pure experience of driving your vehicle in the now. OK, so now what?

Now, exist in the moment like you are riding a wave. Don't try to hang onto the space you're in. Just surrender to the moment and drive. If thoughts arise, notice them, and then bring your attention back to the present moment and let the thought fade. Keep your attention in the now. Your egoic mind is going to try to bring distraction into your field of attention. Let it. Just notice it for what it is and let it go. Keep coming back into the present, silent moment. By silent, I don't mean that there is no sound in your outside environment. Just that there is no sound in your inside environment.

It is this process of noticing distractions and letting them go, then returning to the present moment, that is your practice.

Using this PRND reminder method, I have been able to not only start my practice when first getting in the car in a consistent and precise way, but I have a quick and easy tool to bring myself back into the present moment as I will inevitably have to do. I have also incorporated PRND into my life outside of the vehicle. It is a great way to reset your attention while doing things other than driving your car.

I also noticed that beyond PRND, some vehicles have an L or S for low or sport gears. I offer that these both can represent the same concept, one that is of supreme importance when developing your practice. L is for Let Go and S if for Surrender. It is through this act that we can truly relax in total acceptance of the present moment. If we accept the present moment completely and without reservation, then the thinking mind has no footing in our experience. The thinking, egoic mind needs conflict in order to gain energy. Without it, it has no reason to be. When the egoic mind is faced with acceptance, surrender, and letting go, it collapses onto itself and disappears.

Many times, in my driving practice, when I notice that I am having a hard time staying in the now, if my thoughts are strongly taking my attention or I feel on edge, I remind myself that my practice requires patience. Patience with my progress and myself. I can repurpose the P in PRND to mean patience. I am already intending to practice mindful driving, but I need to first practice patience. If we go back to our definition of patience, we can see that this will require acceptance of what is—delays, trouble, or suffering. It requires acceptance of the reality of our situation without the reactive energy of anger or frustration. We just need to look at that PRND and remind ourselves to be patient, relax, bring our attention into the now, and drive.

No matter how many times we have to do this per trip, we need to remain vigilant of our patience. Without it, we fall into the reactive thinking and emotions that will drive us off course. Often, the observation of these factors that hijack our intention from the present moment are repeated. We can discover that some of biggest distractions from awareness of the current moment are habitual. We notice that we are repeating the same mental mechanisms over and over again. Do not let this frustrate you. It is a great discovery!

We can examine these mechanisms in the light of current moment awareness and find the source of their origin. Often they are based in fear. If I notice that my thoughts are continually being drawn away from the current moment and back to thoughts of an argument I had the previous day, I can stop for a moment and examine where this strong emotional energy is coming from. Am I afraid of being wrong? Was my pride hurt? Am I afraid I will be seen by others as weak or unintelligent? Chances are that whatever the source of the negative energy that has hijacked my attention, it is ego based. I can then recognize that it is a product of my mind, not of reality, and let it go. It may come back. But each time it does come back, it loses a little bit of power until it collapses under the truth of reality as experienced in the current moment. Keep practicing patience.

We can also practice PRND while outside of our cars. While sitting in a waiting room, walking to an appointment, or just about any activity we wish to experience in current moment awareness. All we need to do is think of existing in the current moment as driving our life down the road of life. Our bodies are the vehicles of our being in the physical universe. So, why not use the practicality of PRND in our practice wherever we are? Please, give it a test drive.

CHAPTER 9

TECHNIQUES TO HELP YOU IN YOUR DRIVING PRACTICE

"Your actions are your only true belongings."

— Allan Lokos

I have developed my practice on my own for a period of time. Throughout the evolution of my practice, I have noticed some techniques that have helped me further my experience of mindful driving. I use the word evolution to describe how my practice has developed over time. I think this is an important word in developing an understanding of what happens when we endeavor to practice over time.

—⫷ ⫸—

The Evolution of Humankind

Humans have fallen into thinking behaviors that have led us to believe we *are* what we think. Our egos dictate who we are and the decisions we make. We experience the world through the filter of our egoic, thinking mind. That way of experiencing our lives is not the truth, and it is hampering our evolution as a species. If we can get out of these old thinking patterns through the efforts of our practice, we can evolve and become the species we are meant to be, a species that experiences the reality of the world in which we live and can appreciate it and its inhabitants as valuable members of our collective experience. A species that has the conscious connection to all that is and not just what exists in our own heads. A species that can coexist with not only other species of animals, but our natural environment. We can be the caretakers of the planet instead of the consumers of it. Your practice is a valuable part of the next step in human evolution.

So it is with this idea of evolution that we can look at our own experience in our practice. It should be relaxing and even fun, but it is also very serious. It is a change for the better. We will notice it first in our own lives, and then in the lives of those with whom we associate and interact. They will notice the change in us as well. It is said that when the Buddha attained enlightenment, people who met him noticed there was something about him that seemed different...better. They asked him, "Are you a god?" "No," he replied. "Are you a reincarnation of god?" "No," he replied. "Are you a wizard, then?" "No." "Well, are you a man?" "No." "So, what are you?" They asked, by then quite perplexed. Buddha simply replied, "I am awake."

Let us practice as evolutionaries in a chaotic world. Let us simplify our experience by being in the now. Let us develop our practice for ourselves and for humankind. It sounds lofty, but it is perhaps our most important mission.

Keep the attitude of an evolutionary when you approach practice. It is important! When I feel like I don't want to put forth the effort to practice when I first get into my car, I try to remember that it is important to me. I could just fall into my old way of driving and turn up the music, daydream, talk on the phone, let the chatter in my mind run wild, and miss the true experience of the present moment. But if I can pause and realize the importance of my practice, my mission to relax and experience the truth, it motivates me to take the steps necessary to change my driving habits and work on being present in the moment. I am moved by its importance.

⊨≕⊹ ⊹≔⊨

Plan the Plan

It is also important to not put too many expectations on your driving or your practice. Plan the plan, not the experience. When practicing mindful driving in the present moment, it is important to not have any set end goal for your practice. You must let the experience dictate the practice. Some days, you will not be able to put more than a few seconds of clarity together. Other days, you'll notice longer and longer segments of blissful awareness in the now. Be aware of Truth in your practice. Truth has no judgment, no attachment, and ultimately no resistance. The only resistance will be as a result of egoic thinking. Because your practice will have its own distinct direction and duration, it is important to recognize that and surrender to it. It will change from moment to moment... after all, isn't that the point?

⊨≕⊹ ⊹≔⊨

Easy Does It

I must also caution you against trying to concentrate too hard. It is really not about holding onto concentration focused on one specific thing. We are seeking to hold our attention on the fluid and dynamic now, and any attempt to hold on tightly will result in failure. Mindfulness is not about static concentration, although you will need to practice bringing your attention back from distractions into the present moment awareness that is reality. Mindfulness is about focusing without focus. It is about a dynamic attention that is free and flowing. Once you experience it, you will know it. It can't really be described, but only alluded to. It must be experienced directly.

If you experience doubt as to whether you are or are not really experiencing the now, you must let that go, too. All I can tell you is that if you feel that sweet spot in your practice where you are relaxed, open, serene, without thought of past or future, without labeling or judgment, a very relaxed feeling in your body and mind, you are probably there. If you stay there in the now, often, you will get a sense of mental clarity and heightened awareness, a higher awareness of touch, smells, one's own body, and breath that is not present otherwise. It is important to treat this awareness with a relaxed, unattached demeanor. If you attempt to analyze or define this heightened state of awareness, you will fall away from it. This is where practice over time can vastly improve your experience of awareness and give you a real sense of your being residing in the present moment and not in your thinking mind. You will develop a feeling for when you are in the present and learn not to follow that with thought, but rather experience it as a dynamic reality.

It is just your wide-open attention in the now, unencumbered by your egoic, thinking mind. It really is that simple. Simple but not easy. Only through the direct experience of practice will you be able to know it as the truth. This is where perseverance plays a vital role. Keep practicing, and you will notice that you are indeed learning through your experience. There are periods you might construe as either steps forward or steps backward, good days and days where you feel it is just not working for you. This is normal. This is OK. All of us have experienced that, not only in our practice, but in our lives. We don't expect or strive for any type of perfection in our practice. That would be counterproductive and comes directly from the ego. Try not to judge yourself or your practice too harshly—especially when starting out. An easy, relaxed approach works best.

⊷ ⊶

Clock Time

When you begin your drive, you will probably have a destination in mind such as the store, office, or school. That is fine; it is the reality of daily life. But I would like to introduce the concept of time into the equation and see where it can be a great help to understand our real relationship to time.

There is, of course, "clock time," the time we all agree to observe and put into practice for the purpose of everyone being able to coordinate our lives with each other and the world. Although it doesn't really exist except in our collective minds, it works. We can schedule, meet, make appointments, and synchronize all of the tasks of living with other humans. This is in actuality an agreed upon illusion that works.

Since there is really only now as the one reality, there can be no other than the now. So, there exists no tomorrow at 1:00 p.m. except in our minds. No yesterday morning except how we remember it in our minds. Even through video and photos, we are looking at an image as it exists only in the now. This might sound a little esoteric to some, but at its deepest root, it is the truth.

That being said...if you try to keep the concept of clock time in your mind while practicing awareness of the present moment, you are working against yourself. If one sits in meditation and sets a timer for thirty minutes, then only thinks of the time that the chime will sound, they have spent thirty minutes in their minds thinking of the future and no time in the present moment with full awareness.

The same holds true for your driving practice. Of course, if you are on your way to work and need to be there by 9:00 a.m. to keep your job, then it is important to get there on time…clock time. It is a good idea when developing a mindfulness practice to leave a few minutes early to avoid any tension that could develop with clock time anxiety. If you're looking at the clock and getting worked up about not making it on time, you have created a poor environment for relaxing and being able to practice. So, get into your vehicle with a few extra minutes to spare in the interest of eliminating "clock time" on your drive. If you arrive early, you can always sit in quiet contemplation of your experience and feel the calm, relaxed state you are in. What a great way to start the work day!

Once you actually start practicing, time will no longer be relevant as it relates to your state of awareness. You are focusing on the present moment and as there is only now; clock time does not come into play. That is not to say you are unaware of the common conception of clock time, just that you are choosing to put all of your attention on the present and therefore have no need for clock time except to manage your day-to-day affairs. It really is quite liberating. Surrendering to the moment is in itself quite liberating, and diminishing the power of clock time is only one facet of this liberation.

<hr/>

Destination Now

Know where you are going…kind of. Many of us live a life of destination addiction. We are firmly convinced that the happiness we seek is just one step further in the future with the next job, relationship, or home. We live a life of grass that is always greener. Unfortunately, that grass doesn't really exist because it is only in our minds. What really exists is the now. We have to learn to let go of the idea that our only path to happiness is somewhere other than right here, right now. If we stick with the old programmed way of thinking, we can never be happy where we are. So plan the plan, but not the outcome.

In other words, have a good idea of where you want to go and how you are going to get there, but do not expect this plan to go perfectly. It might, but that will unfold as you proceed in the present moment.

A lot of anxiety is created when we are firmly wrapped up in our expectations. Remember, the plan is just your idea of what may happen, not the reality of what *is* happening. Anytime you have expectations of the future, you are at risk of creating anxiety when things go differently in reality than they did in your mind. If you go forward with the attitude that all you can really experience is in the now and acknowledge that the now is forever dynamic, you will not be upset when the dynamism of life is demonstrated to you over and over again. In other words, expect the unexpected.

It is also important to not be totally attached to your planned route. Although a planned or familiar route to a destination can make us feel more comfortable, if we need to alter that route, it can make us very uncomfortable. Being totally in the present moment will sometimes take us out of our comfort zone while demanding that we stay present and connected. If you have to take a detour or an alternate route for whatever reason, just make that a part of your journey in the now. You may be surprised at how pleasant a new path can be.

⚔ ⚔

Space and Time

Although concepts in our intelligent, thinking mind are important for planning, problem solving, and learning, do not get hung up on the concepts of space and time. It is interesting that there is no reality to our direct experience except in this second and in this exact place. We can conceive of other times, past and future, and other places where we are not, but those are only constructs of the mind and do not exist to us directly in this moment. Is it any wonder that we cannot comprehend the boundaries of space and time? We call it the space/time continuum. If we are to view this concept in our only true reality (the now), we can see that the totality of time and space do not really exist except in our minds.

Does our concept of clock time exist in our minds only as a unidirectional flowing measure of moments? Are space and time interwoven, and do they even exist outside of the mind? These are questions that humans have been pondering for centuries—but they are not any part of our direct experience in the present moment. They do not matter to your present moment experience. In fact, such concepts of the mind only serve to distract us from direct experience.

━┿ ┿━

In the Laboratory

I try to look at my car as a laboratory for cultivating mindful experience. I experiment on myself using my practice. I find out what works for me and what does not. I learn what cultivates patience, compassion, and serenity. I experience the pitfalls of my own thinking and emotional patterns and learn to recognize them for what they are. I find my own way, in my own practice, in my own time. By using my time behind the wheel in this way, I learn the truth about myself.

━┿ ┿━

Snap Back to Reality

If I am having a particularly hard time relaxing into the present moment, I can use the technique of visualization to bring myself into it. Kind of a jump-start or a snapback. For whatever reason, I sometimes have a very hard time entering the state of awareness in the present moment. My thoughts or emotions are particularly strong that day, or maybe I am anxious or tired. I reset my intention and relaxation and then visualize watching myself from outside my vehicle, either above or to the side. I see myself driving my car down the road. Then I snap my attention back into my body and get the sense that I am right here, right now, inside my skin. I may have to do this several times, but usually, it helps right away.

⟞⟝ ⟞⟝

Surrender to Yourself

It is also important for me to understand that at times, I will be fighting myself, and then I must learn to recognize internal conflict and handle it. By surrendering to the reality of my own imperfect way of being, I can recognize my human condition and work with it to bring about the transformation I am seeking. What do I mean? I wrote in a previous chapter about surrendering to the ego by recognizing it and bringing your attention away from it and back into the now in order to collapse it. When I feel that conflict of internal contradiction, I know it is time to put acceptance and surrender into practice, then redirect my attention into the now to dissolve the power of that conflict. In doing this on a repeated basis every time I experience that type of inner conflict in my practice, I can more easily recognize it and access the remedy in my time away from my driving practice. In other words, I learn to experience practice outside of my driving practice. That is where the true rewards of the transformation take place.

It is my intention when getting out of the car to carry my practice with me everywhere I go and in everything I do. My driving practice is my laboratory, a safe place where I can develop my mindfulness through driving in the present moment. The outside world is where I can put my practice into practice. Meditators might describe this as time on the cushion (practice) and time off the cushion (practicing what we have experienced on the cushion out in the world). Once we leave the confines of our car, we are still in the present moment. We can still practice present moment awareness, patience, compassion, and serenity. Notice your experience as you exit your car and close the door. As you walk, work, eat, speak, breathe, and even sleep. This is the key to transforming awareness of your reality. If we kept it all in the car, we would be very mindful drivers indeed. However, it is our intention to become mindful human beings and experience our lives in the reality of the present moment. That is the true transformative power of our practice.

Practice demands that we free ourselves from concepts of the mind in order to fully experience the now. We realize that our intelligence is perhaps our most valuable tool as humans. Our practice does not seek to eliminate thoughts and concepts, but rather to slowly reveal to us that they are not who we are. By practicing our current moment awareness, we come to experience our real spiritual being—the essence of who and what we truly are. With this experience and realization come serenity and the peace of knowing the Truth.

Overcoming Perceived Problems

Many times, we encounter what we consider to be problems or roadblocks to a smooth practice. This is common, experienced by everyone who practices in earnest, and is actually an expected part of your practice. It is important to recognize these "problems" as an opportunity to improve and strengthen your practice and not as a difficult frustration that is keeping you from developing a good practice. While it might feel like this at first, I have discovered for myself that these difficulties are sometimes the biggest opportunities to go deeper into my practice, if I can recognize them for what they are, don't let them stop me, and approach them with the right attitude.

If we attempt to avoid these problems or deny them to ourselves as we have with other problems in our lives, we will be stuck in the same mental pattern that we experienced in the first place. In our driving practice, we can examine these problems in the laboratory of our current moment awareness and discover not only their power but their solution as well. Avoiding them in our practice only gives them power, and they will come back even stronger. Face them directly. Surrender to them. Take away their power by withdrawing attention from them and directing it back to the reality of the present moment. If they keep coming, recognize them again, then move your attention back to reality. They will be revealed as manifestations of the mind and can be treated realistically and accordingly.

Be patient with yourself and your initial reactions to these problems and the thoughts and feeling that may come up. By facing them directly, we learn to recognize them and mindfully learn their way rather than fear them. Keep in mind that you are not alone. Everyone who is courageous enough to endeavor to practice mindfulness in the present moment will have to deal with the same issues as you. Just know that if you are steadfast in your commitment to practice, things will become clear, and you will make the necessary adjustments to your practice and your way of seeing how your egoic mind functions. Above all, you will learn that you are not your egoic mind, with all of its conflicts, judgments, and anxieties. You are your higher self, the observer of the mind, the present moment reality, the divine.

⇒+ +⇐

Overcoming Mood

Sometimes, we may not feel that we are in the right mood to practice mindful driving. Maybe we woke up on the wrong side of the bed.

Perhaps the events of the day have left us in a sour mood. This is an opportunity to jump in with both feet and put our practice into real action. Can we overcome this? Can we mindfully examine our state of mind in the present moment? Not try to avoid it or deny it, just feel it directly, see it for what it is, and diminish its power over us? One thing is sure, those feelings are not permanent and will change. Being aware of them and feeling the change take place can be revealing and liberating. Maybe you are tired. Maybe you can't put your finger on it. It can feel like a tightness in your body. When you push to get away from it, it becomes stronger. They key is to surrender to it. Really feel and observe it. Breathe and surrender. Let it go and pay attention to the now. Repeat this process as necessary.

If you feel tension in your physical body, be sure to scan your muscles for tension and relax them. Feel your hands on the steering wheel and be sure they are light and relaxed. Check your upper back, neck, and shoulders, they are notorious for storing tension in our bodies—especially while driving. Relax your legs and feel your feet in your shoes touching the floor of the car. Anywhere you scan and feel tension, recognize it and relax. Let go and refocus your attention on the now. Your body and mind are intricately linked. When one is tense, chances are the other is as well. Feel the link, relax both components of that link, and create a relaxed unity in your body. You may have to scan and relax multiple times. Be patient and do not give in to mental frustration. Treat the tension as if it were a child that needs to be nurtured and bathed in awareness.

＊＜＋＋＞＊

Overcoming Boredom

If you feel yourself becoming bored in your practice, again, you are not alone. It is something every one of us will have to deal with. We are used to amusing our egoic mind with its own little movies of past and future, distractions, and fantasies. Couple those thought movies with the corresponding feelings and emotions they can conjure up in our bodies, and they create an all-consuming show for our attention. Once it is revealed that these thoughts and emotions are not based on reality, we are freed from the deception, but also from the excitement they produced in our mind and body. Although, with time, you will find that there is no excitement like the present moment, your ego does not want to accept this. It will be bored. Recognize your sense of boredom as emanating from the ego. Recommit yourself in mindfulness to the present moment, and stay aware. This is the true essence of practice.

You may also notice the same type of phenomenon manifesting itself as drowsiness, especially when you are a beginner. If we are not used to being relaxed and calm, our mind/body may interpret our relaxed state as a sign that we need to sleep. Watch this closely and become aware of how it manifests in you. Do your eyes become heavy? Do you start yawning? Direct the sharp lens of present moment awareness on your drowsiness, and you will see it diminish. If you really are tired and need sleep, it would be prudent to get off the road. Be sure to get proper sleep and physical rest in order to facilitate a functional practice.

⊱━⊰ ⊱━⊰

Experiencing Fear

Many times in practice, we feel a tinge of fear as we experience the present moment. This is usually due to some part of our ego rising up and fearing the intensity of the truth in the present moment. We may at first feel as if we are letting go of what kept us feeling safe and grounded. This can be thought of as releasing the chains of bondage and feeling the lightness without them. It may feel unnatural at first.

In that way, we may feel paradoxically uncomfortable with being comfortable. We need to observe that feeling, put it in the context of our practice, and proceed with courage and the knowledge that we are making progress. Above all, do not ignore it, and conversely, do not give it the power to deter you in your practice. This is where the courage component of practice comes in. Be brave. You will be fine. Remember, most progress takes place out of your comfort zone.

If you are agitated, restless, or maybe just trying too hard, you need to back up, reset, PRND, and move forward with your practice. It is just another moment in the laboratory of your driving practice. All of these feelings are leftover manifestations of the old way of being. They do not disappear overnight, and probably will not disappear 100 percent ever. They are a part of the human condition. It is important that they are dealt with in a mindful, calm, and thoughtful way so that we can make progress in our practice. They are, in fact, the fodder for our practice and progress.

Do not be discouraged by these problems. If mindful driving and living were easy, everyone would be doing it without effort and the world would be a much more serene place. But this is not the case. Recommit yourself on a daily basis to your driving practice; do not resist the problems that arise, your practice is dynamic and always changing. What holds true for today may not be your experience tomorrow. Expect the unexpected and do not think of these issues as setbacks. As long as you are mindful and conscious of the moment no matter what it holds, you will continue to learn. Be sure to think of them as opportunities, and if treated as such, they will become just that!

〜✦✦〜

Dealing with Self-Doubt

Sometimes, we may feel just plain discouraged with the whole practice in general. We may feel that we are not very good at it. We may think we are not getting anywhere and putting all of this effort in for no reason. I too have felt like this. In fact, I'm willing to wager that everyone who has put forth the intention to practice on a serious level has experienced this. Doubt is part of the journey. That is your ego saying, "See...I told you it wouldn't work. Come back to your old way of being with me."

Don't buy it. You have probably heard the old adage "It works if you work it, so work it, you're worth it." That applies to your driving practice as well. If you don't buy into the doubt, whether it's self-doubt, doubt of the process, or doubt that there is anything wrong with your old egoic way of being, just take a step back and reexamine your place in the process. This is supposed to happen. You are supposed to encounter doubt...probably a number of times. Sometimes, it will be a brief feeling of uneasiness with your practice; other times, it will stop you dead in your tracks and make you question why you even pursued it in the first place.

Don't take all of this too seriously. Remember, progress is dynamic too. Sometimes fast, sometimes slow, sometimes not at all. It has been my experience that when dealing with a bout of doubt, it is important to know that everything is going to be OK. This too shall pass. You are in good company. Your driving practice is a moment by moment entity. It is incremental in that every moment contains in it the one moment—now. It is to be expected that your egoic thinking is going to try to derail its own diminishment by introducing doubt into your thinking. If you take a step back, reset, PRND, and surrender to doubt in your practice, you will be fine.

After all, is serenity the absence of all doubt, all problems, or all conflict? No. If that were the case, no one would ever have serenity in their life. Serenity is found in surrender, acceptance, and unity with what is. If you encounter a problem and it is not within your power to change it at that moment, you can accept it, surrender to the fact that it cannot be changed at that moment, and seek unity with the reality of it. Then you can experience serenity even though the problem still exists. If you wait for all your problems, conflicts, and doubt to disappear, you will never know serenity.

━◈━ ━◈━

The Suspension of Thinking

Sometimes you may feel that you just can't stop thinking. The idea of practice is to suspend mental egoic thought and experience the present moment with all of your awareness. If you are thinking, your awareness is on the thoughts that are produced by your own mind, your imagination, and your ego. In order to get back on track in your driving practice, it is important to move your awareness away from your egoic mind and suspend the thought in order to experience the moment directly.

Find something in the present moment—it can be the horizon, your speedometer, the clouds in the sky, the feeling of your hands on the wheel, anything that is happening or can be experienced right now. Focus your attention on that experience and just be aware of it without quantifying, judging, or thinking about it. You may have to restart your focus several times. You may have to move from one thing to another in the present moment to help hold your attention. The idea is to get yourself to recognize that you are in the present moment and only in the present moment.

The thinking mind is used to changing very quickly from thought or image to a new or different thought or image. It might be helpful at first to allow your awareness of the present moment to experience the same mechanism to ease the transition away from the thought engulfed mind. Then you will notice that the speed at which you observe and experience focus in the present will begin to slow down on its own. Your breathing may slow down. Pause and reset your relaxation; keep slowing down. It's all about attention. If you try to stop your mind from focusing on mental thoughts, you only strengthen its hold. By moving attention into the present moment, the mental thoughts lose their hold and dissolve. It is in this way we rescue our attention from our egoic minds.

This chapter outlines only a few experiences and techniques in the practice of mindful driving. As your own practice develops, you will find what works for you. The experience of having situations that test our intended practice is what the practice is. When we encounter the egoic mind and notice its characteristics, we can then begin to affect the change in our own way of being and evolve into the people we are meant to be.

CHAPTER 10

THE ESOTERIC CHAPTER

"We too should make ourselves empty, that the great soul of the universe may fill us with its breath."

— Laurence Binyon

In the chapter Hocus Pocus vs. Mumbo Jumbo, it was made clear that this was not a book about the esoteric aspects of spirituality but rather a guide to developing a practice through mindfulness while driving, and some of the reasons for pursuing this as a practice.

There are, however, some esoteric type concepts that may help some people. I am going to write about a few of them in this chapter. So, if this isn't for you...feel free to skip it. If you do decide to read it, just be open to the ideas and try not to jump to judgment. Sometimes, ideas are best understood as subtle truths rather than literal truths.

In my experience, the nature of spirituality is the same for everyone as it is experienced. That oneness, unity, serenity, peace, understanding, connection, whatever you choose to call it, is our experiential connection to who we are beyond thoughts, emotions, conditions, and concepts. Just as the experience of the now is interrupted as soon as our egoic, thinking mind creeps into our awareness, the truth of the experience is interrupted as soon as we try to define it, explain it, or even describe it. So then, how can we talk about it? We cannot talk about it in any definite terms. We can only allude to it, point to it, or talk about our relationship to it as it exists in our egoic mind. For instance, we might tell someone that when we are fully present in the now, we experience a lightness of being or a warm comfort in our bodies. That is really describing our reaction to the experience, not the experience itself. We can also say that our minds are clear and relaxed, our emotions calm. While that may be true to us as we remember how we felt during the experience, it is far from the actual experience of being in the now.

It cannot be experienced other than by experiencing it yourself. It is beyond words, concepts, descriptions, and logic. It simply is an experience. For me, this experience is the experience of God or becoming my true self in God. There are no words or concepts in the experience. In fact, as soon as they are introduced, they diminish or extinguish the experience. Therefore, it is highly personal. Yet at the same time, I realize in the experience that I am connected to everything. What could be less personal? So it is, in fact, holding to the old saying, "Those that tell don't know, and those that know can't tell." Although it might seem like I am telling, I am not. I can't. What I am saying is that it has to be experienced. I can only point you to the road; you will have to walk it yourself to go anywhere.

I was talking to a friend of mine once about religions of the world and how they are all experiencing the same spiritual reality, but from different cultures, histories, teachings, and attitudes, so they describe it differently. They try to use their egoic minds to "teach" the experience to others through the lens of their experiences and the teachings they received. When someone is indoctrinated into these teachings and has a spiritual experience, the teachings are given absolute validity in the minds of the practitioner and therefore are taken as the truth, often as the only one real way or truth. When confronted with other ideologies and religious concepts, they cry foul and feel to their deepest soul that their experience validates their religion, so the others are just plain wrong.

My friend offered, as he held his cell phone up to me, that we were both looking at the same phone. Me from the back, him from the front. If we were asked to describe the phone, we would have two totally different descriptions in our minds, with few similarities, and we would both be right—from our point of view or orientation. Same phone, same experience, with a different orientation. He was right.

And so I feel it is the same with different religions or faiths of the world. We are all connecting to the same truth (reality) but are couching it in our egoic, thinking mind through the lens of what we have learned, thought, or felt about the experience. Therein lies the error. Once our egoic mind is introduced into the picture, the uncluttered truth becomes obscured. There is still truth there, it is just obscured. What if we don't filter the spiritual with words, concepts, and descriptions? What if we leave the earthly absolutes and dogma out of it? What if we bask in the experience of Truth and look to our fellow humans and know that they are experiencing the same truth, void of thought? We are all one race, one world, one existence, one Truth. How could it be any other way?

With the experience of being fully in the now, we are in fact experiencing what it is to be our true selves. Our essence or true nature uncluttered by the thinking, egoic mind is recognized as our only true reality. Since it is the only true reality, and unencumbered by dogma or thought, it will fit with any path of spirituality that seeks to know God. Rather, it will not conflict with the teachings or tenets of any religion, tradition, or faith since it only holds the experience of spirit and none of the boundaries or definitions of spiritual traditions. There should be no conflict with your chosen spiritual path in experiencing the now through your practice. In fact, it has a great potential to deepen and enhance your spiritual practices, no matter what they are.

In the past, I have pondered the eternal questions of humankind. Why are we here? What are we? What are we supposed to do? I have yet to get any definitive answers that work for me. The problem is, I am asking myself those questions in the limited realm of my thinking mind. To find the answers to the eternal questions, I must seek the eternal within myself. That is the eternal now. Once I have reached awareness in the now, the questions dissolve, and the answers are experienced. Can I recite the answers to you now? No, I cannot. They are not answers that can be recognized by the thinking mind, words, or explanations. They are answers that can only be experienced.

It is by practicing awareness in the now that we arrive at the answers to the questions that have no answer in the realm of thought. The interesting thing about the experience is that the answers are always there just waiting to be realized through awareness. Once the obstruction of mind is cleared, they are recognized fully and easily. I encourage you to practice using PRND with the intention of clearing the obstruction of the egoic mind and experiencing your pure awareness in the now. If there ever were answers to be found to the esoteric questions of mankind, the realm of the spirit in the now is a great place to experience them.

Probably the biggest positive change that can come out of developing a conscious driving practice is that your higher self is revealed to you. I think that by some definition, this is true of all meditative practices. Once the burden of egoic thinking is minimized or removed for a period of time, a clarity emerges that contains within it a connectedness and serenity. This is your true self, or your higher self. It hasn't been manufactured as a result of your practice. It has been revealed. It was there all the time. It is the Real You.

I have found trying to define the experience of being my higher self not only impossible, but a complete and utter waste of time. It can only be experienced without the egoic mind. Any attempt to define it is a product of the egoic mind and, therefore, sorely lacking.

Once you experience it, you will only then know what I am writing about. I can't tell you what it is because it is *you*, and only you know the true self that is you. I can spend a lot of time telling you what it is not. It is not what the ego would have you believe is the Real You. It doesn't judge, exclude, hate, boast, or any of the other things that the egoic mind would have you believe your true self does. It also doesn't soar in victory, revel in material accomplishment, or beam with pride at success. It does not recognize victory and defeat, increase and decrease, or birth and death. It is pure consciousness and can only be experienced in the present moment. It is timeless (since it doesn't recognize clock time); it is ageless (after all, what age is now?); and it is always present (as in this moment).

So, there it is…now what? Well, if you dwell as your higher self for any amount of time, you will notice that you are connected to everything and nothing. The Buddhists say, "Form is emptiness. Emptiness is form." Within this realm is where the Truth resides. So how does that help us live in this world? It reveals the truth.

What truth? The whole truth and nothing but the truth, so help me God—or higher self! When accessing our higher self, we will know the truth without effort. When something you are doing or thinking doesn't seem 100 percent right, or may in some way be questionable, a good question to ask yourself is, "Does this serve my higher self?" When this question is followed by silence and attention in the now, it will bring knowing. Once the egoic mind is removed from the equation, the truth is revealed.

Some of you may be thinking, "So, what am I supposed to do, question every decision I ever make? This sounds a lot like self-doubt to me, and I already suffer from enough of that." Is this self-doubt? No. It is ego doubt. You see, real self-doubt means doubting your true self. It is your ego nagging you, telling you, you don't know what you're doing, that you're a failure, and you make bad choices. And because you have failed and made bad choices before, you believe it. The ego's trick is that it was, in fact, the ego itself that influenced those bad decisions and then put the blame squarely on your shoulders! Now it is using its own poor decision-making influence to trick you into making even poorer decisions; or at least if you make the right decision, see you wallow in the misery of self-doubt while doing it. Is this any way to live? I think not!

Being your higher self means being who you always really are without the obstruction of ego. This is no easy task. So, why does the ego do this? Because it doesn't really exist and needs to keep putting itself in front of you so that you think it does. It gains strength from conflict, anxiety, self-doubt, pride, just about anything you can think of that reduces serenity in your life. Somewhere along the lines of human evolution, people began to think that the immense gift of our intelligent mind was, in fact, who we are. This is the problem. We are spiritual beings having a human experience. Not human beings who sometimes have spiritual experiences. Over hundreds of generations, our true selves have been obscured by our thinking minds as our ego has grown to lord over our lives. I believe it is the next step in the evolutionary process to transcend the egoic mind and become our true selves. You are a part of that evolution.

When we practice mindful driving and enter into the present moment completely, we become our higher selves. By becoming our higher selves, I mean that the truth of who we really are is revealed to our conscious mind through attention to the experience of being in the moment—the Truth. We can then bring that clarity, serenity, and natural compassion out into the world, and into all areas of our life. It is hard to keep that clarity for any amount of time without distraction. This is the state of our being as humans today, so it is going to take conscious effort—work!

The more we work on our practice, the more we are able to dwell in the Truth. It is easy to slip back into our old way of egoic thinking. That is our comfort zone. When I began a regular practice in my driving, it seemed as though I was feeling more uncomfortable in my own skin for a bit. This is natural. It is our ego's way of trying to fight back. It gives us an extra dose of self-doubt as it tries to work its way back into the forefront of our attention. Recognize it for what it is and continue to practice.

When you view your egoic mind from the standpoint of the detached observer, you learn to recognize its tricks. You can see the way your mind works and just watch it without reacting. The ego loses strength when you do this, and the egoic thought fades away. Just be a vigilant observer of your own thoughts and emotions, and you will notice the ego's patterns. If you react to egoic thinking, you strengthen the ego, you give it energy. If you observe and do not react, the ego gains no energy and collapses on itself. Just be aware that it will keep trying.

It may seem like you are doing battle with yourself. This is not what you want. If you are doing battle with your ego, you strengthen it. When I first recognized my ego as being distinct from my true self, it felt as if I was living with the enemy inside my head. What a terrible feeling. The ego was strong and gaining strength as I tried to fight it. When I realized that the phenomenon of ego was a *part* of my human makeup, I had to come to terms with the fact it wasn't going anywhere. I had to understand that my ego was a part of me. What I sought was an understanding and unity through the experience of knowing my higher self and working with the phenomenon of egoic mind through my practice. Once you truly realize what your egoic mind is and is not, you can learn to coexist with it in peace. Keep it in check by realizing the truth, and find unity within yourself to bring about a lasting serenity and understanding. These may seem life lofty goals, and perhaps they are. But isn't that what change is all about? Work, action, understanding, learning, and realizing the truth?

So, what's the point of the whole exercise? What is the idea or change we hope to see?

All we are trying to do is clear that which would obscure the ever-present, eternal now that is the only truth. What do we hope to do once we are there? Just be. Dwell in the Truth. Observe the gaps between thoughts, and experience the now. It is here that we connect with our true self and find peace, serenity, and freedom.

If you have never experienced what I am referring to, you may think it is just an unattainable goal. It is not. It is totally attainable and always there for you to access. As I have stated throughout this book, it cannot be adequately described. It has to be experienced. Through your practice of mindful driving, you can calm your mind, relax your body, and create an internal environment conducive to experiencing the now that I am referring to. At first, it comes in tiny intervals between mental thoughts and images. A small space between our mind's concepts and judgments. With time and practice, the space between thoughts becomes longer and deeper. When you experience this, you may find the comfort you feel is in knowing that this is your true nature, the Real You.

Connection to the mind, emotions, and the old you begin to lose their grip on your self-identification. The inner stillness of being in the now reveals the Real You. The experience of being in the now will bring more and more inner understanding of the Truth. Creativity, intelligence beyond the egoic mind, serenity, peace, and love emanate from this vast and timeless realm. It is in this state that we can truly exist as we were meant to be.

Once we are able to recognize the egoic mind for what it is, and we are able to make sense of our existence in this world as human beings living as one with all there is, we can be free of the disease of the compulsively thinking mind. We can use our intelligence as a decision-making tool instead of allowing it to devolve into the ego, which masked our true identity. It is from this point that we can awaken and live as liberated beings.

By simply beginning and following our practice, we can open up a whole new life for ourselves. A life of compassion, patience, empathy, conscious presence, and ultimately, joy. I am not trying to put forth the notion that all conflict and problems will disappear from life. Rather, your ability to deal with what comes along in life will be vastly improved through your experience of knowing the truth about yourself. Even if your life improves a few percentage points, isn't that worth doing? There is also the possibility that if you continue to develop your practice in more areas of your life, things can vastly improve for you.

Fear, anxiety, and destructive thoughts can be minimized or eliminated. Relationships can improve and become filled with understanding, compassion, and joy. Inner connectedness brings with it a confidence, not of ego, but of humility. An energy free of fear and void of selfishness. This will become evident not only in your way of thinking, but in the way you interact with others. It brings with it respect and a certain attraction for others to interact with you on an honest, intelligent level. Practice also develops within you a sense of how better to understand and help others. You will feel the pure joy of helping selflessly and knowing that you are truly an agent of the ever-advancing creation that is the current moment.

Practice can be not only a pivotal starting point to having a more serene drive to work in the morning, it can transform your entire life and the lives of those around you. If others notice a positive change in your demeanor and behavior, you can share your experiences with them and help them start a change of their own. This is the grassroots of the revolution of evolution. Practice your mindfulness outside of your car. When you walk, feel the bottoms of your feet on the earth. When you shower in the morning, feel the water on your body, its temperature, the scent of your shampoo on your hair, notice what is happening in the now without judgment. Carry this gift with you.

CHAPTER 11

COMPASSIONATE DRIVING... THE KEY

"A human being is a part of the whole called by us universe, a part limited in time and space. He experiences himself, his thoughts and feeling as something separated from the rest, a kind of optical delusion of his consciousness. This delusion is a kind of prison for us, restricting us to our personal desires and to affection for a few persons nearest to us. Our task must be to free ourselves from this prison by widening our circle of compassion to embrace all living creatures and the whole of nature in its beauty."

—Albert Einstein

What we intend to transform through our practice is ourselves. We apply our practice through our driving experience and use our car as a vehicle for liberation from the thinking, egoic mind. We intend to exit our car in a different mindset than when we entered it to begin our trip. This is the basis of our evolution through practice. We intend to join the revolution of living in the now as the next step of our personal evolution and so the evolution of our species.

You may be asking yourself if evolution only happens through natural selection. If that is the case, please realize that you selected to read this book, selected to begin a practice to transform yourself, and hopefully will select to continue your practice and share what you have found with others. Natural selection. You may also have realized by now that this approach to transformation is not for everyone. Some will reject these ideas out of hand as just another new age, self-help gimmick. Others will understand its value but decide that it won't work for them without even trying it. Still others will try it and then give up, perhaps deciding it was too much effort or the results weren't coming fast enough.

These are all legitimate reactions to the idea of developing a practice of mindfulness, whether driving in a car or sitting on a cushion. It is not for everyone. It does take effort. It takes uncomfortable adjustment, frustration, and self-doubt. That is all part of the process, and many people are just not there yet. Those of us who seek an answer to our human condition do so out of a need to seek the relief of Truth. Pain is our motivator. Feeling uncomfortable in our own skin or in our own car is what pushes us to seek change and formulate a plan for how to go about it. If this is you, you have chosen the right path.

We are taught very early on in our lives that we must compete to get what we want out of life. This may be true for the ego to get what it wants out of life—money, prestige, social standing, material objects, etc. But most of us realize at some point that is not what we really want out of life. What we really want is security, love, meaning, clarity, and the sense that we matter and make a difference. So we need to realize that the driving force making us competitive in our current mindset is the ego. Once we realize this in a profound way, we will recognize it immediately when it tries to dominate our motivations and actions.

We can pull back and watch the thoughts and feelings develop and realize them for what they are. We can ask ourselves if these courses of action truly serve our higher self. We know from experience that satisfying the ego is always short lived and hollow and leads ultimately to feelings of longing and frustration. We spend a lot of time in our heads thinking, "When this next thing happens...then I'll be happy." When we get that raise/spouse/home/retirement/etc., then we can finally be happy. Then, when we arrive at our destination, we still end up with that same sense of being unfulfilled. This is because our egoic mind is not the truth. It is not who we truly are.

As children, we are taught to compete and that this competition is necessary for us to survive in the existing social climate of the human race. What we eventually learn is that if we want to be truly fulfilled, we need to look to our higher self for a different way of being. Our higher self will tell us that the way to fulfill our destiny as humans is not through competition, but through cooperation. Cooperation with the reality of life in the present moment, cooperation with our fellow human beings, and cooperation with our higher self, which is a part of the whole of the universe. This is the way to serenity, happiness, and peace.

Your driving practice is an excellent way to test, evaluate, and learn the way of cooperation. In fact, driving would not be able to exist if it were not for cooperation. We all need to understand and respect the rules of the road in order for the flow of traffic to work. If we didn't have cooperation on the use of lanes, traffic signs, direction of traffic, and all of the other rules of the road that make safe driving possible, we would have chaos. In the realm of safe driving, cooperation, and compassion, we can accomplish together what would be impossible to create in a world of competition and ego-driven selfishness.

Imagine if there were no stop signs and everyone just blew through every intersection or drove whichever way they felt down either side of the road? It would make it impossible to drive anywhere safely. Driving as we know it would end. Cooperation is the basis of driving, and it is cooperation that we seek to cultivate in our own driving—and in our lives.

Cooperation on the road doesn't mean being a doormat for aggressive drivers. We aren't looking to drive as people pleasers, going out of our way to acquiesce to other drivers. What we are looking to do is to drive and act as our higher selves. We have driven as ego-motivated drivers for far too long. The ego seeks to expand the divide between us and others drivers by judging and trying to control how the other drivers on the road are allowed to act.

Many of us drive with the egoic mindset as if we own the road. Our first reaction to what we perceive as any kind of violation of that idea is to take exception to that driver. We may think, "How dare they drift into my lane (drive too slow or too fast for me, change lanes too much for me, not change lanes enough for me, or not get out of my way)! After all, I own the road!" We probably don't actually think those words, but we may react as if that is genuinely how we feel. It can trigger in our behavior actions that seek to set the other driver straight, putting them in their place, winning a race with them, or passing judgment on them. This is not only toxic to the other drivers on the road, it is particularly toxic to ourselves. It keeps us from the truth of our higher selves and seeks to keep us from the truth of realizing that we are a part of a higher humanity that thrives on cooperation and withers in division.

This is where cooperation leads to integration and unity with all of existence. These, of course, are esoteric concepts and only serve to describe the experience of being compassionate in the now. This sense of harmony and serenity is sublime and exists for those who practice to experience it. For those who don't, it is still there and always will be, even though it is shrouded from view by the ego.

We feel self-righteous and revel in an opportunity to put what we consider "bad drivers" in their place. This results in us becoming the bad driver we seek to correct through our punishment and ultimately punishes us by keeping us from the truth about ourselves. It is important when another driver reacts to us in an egoic way that we are able to recognize it immediately and also recognize their reaction as a potential in ourselves. It is then we can act from the seat of the higher self and drive with compassion.

The Bible talks about turning the other cheek. I think this alludes to realizing that the person who is striking us or competing with us has not yet realized the truth about cooperation and compassion and is still chasing the dream of the ego. We may think that since their behavior is unacceptable to us, we should straighten them out. In doing this, we actually affirm their actions by competing with them in offering a reprisal. By accepting them and their behavior with gentle compassion, we stand as a living testament to the truth of cooperation.

If someone cuts you off in traffic, you may want to rethink laying on the horn, swearing at them, and flipping them off. Chances are they will return your behavior in kind, and the ego has thus won. Instead, recognize that person in yourself. You too have made mistakes, and chances are you have cut someone off in error sometime in your life. Give them a smile, a pleasant wave, and let them be on their way. There will be no ill feelings created, no negative energy born, and in fact, you will feel good about being able to exercise your higher self in a situation where you might have acted otherwise had you not been a compassionate driver. I have found myself smiling when this has been my experience.

However, we are not to be doormats for aggressive drivers. If you feel that someone is driving so aggressively that they pose a real danger, back away from them and let them pass. Note the make, model, and perhaps license plate number of the vehicle and contact the authorities. You may be saving a life. The majority of conflict on the road is totally avoidable with a little compassion and cooperation. This is especially true of road rage incidents.

When I am driving from a compassionate mindset, I am relaxed, focused, and mentally at ease. I am not out to race anyone, repeatedly switch lanes to make better time, or speed in excess of the posted speed limit. In fact, when I was first developing my practice, I would notice that when I was in my relaxed, focused state, I would have to check my speedometer to make sure I was going the speed limit. The road seemed to slow down to me. The feeling of rushing was diminished. The calm of the present moment transformed my environment and mental condition into a slower, more serene experience.

When I exit my vehicle, I take that with me. Sometimes for a long time, sometimes not. The important thing is that I have cleared away the ego and experienced the Truth. Through diligent practice, that Truth becomes more and more a reality in my life. I can not only drive with compassion and serenity, I can walk with compassion and serenity. I can feel my feet inside my shoes walking the earth, be in the moment as I walk down the sidewalk. I can eat, work, breathe, and exist in the present moment and live the Truth. What could be better? And all because I made the choice to practice with intention to drive in the now.

The change in your attitude toward others on the road and in your life will come in subtle ways at first. One way to help this change occur is to realize that we are all in this together. Even the aggressive driver is a member of our driving community. It is important that we take the "I" out of our driving and replace it with "we," "us," and "our." Safe travel on the road only exists if we all buy into this cooperation. If we can take away the attitude of "I" and "they," or "me" and "them" and look upon others as a part of the "we" on the road, we can shatter the illusion of separateness as it relates to our driving experience. By finding unity on the road with all other drivers, we can cultivate compassion and unity with all other beings in life.

This may sound like a tall order. In the past, we have all encountered aggressive jerks, bad drivers, and just plain inconsiderate behavior behind the wheel. This is where humility comes into play. We must come from the place of our higher self in order to be humble in the face of things that would normally antagonize our egos. For most of us, this is going to take some getting used to. We are not perfect either. Let he who is without fault cast the first stone. We have all been guilty at one time or another of being imperfect on the road. Again, when you encounter this type of behavior, step back, reset, and relax into your humble higher self.

I have had this experience many times on the road. Someone cuts me off or lays on the horn for me to get out of their way so they can speed by me, or flips me off for a reason that is still unclear to me. My first reactive feeling is to retaliate, escalate, and set them straight. I don't want to be pushed around, and I'm going to stick up for myself. I have found that when I just relax and smile at them, let them pass, or offer a friendly wave, it brings a genuine smile to my face. Sometimes it even makes me laugh out loud as I go on my merry way. Why? Because it is not how I am used to reacting. In my old way of thinking, I would have experienced anger, anxiety, resentment, and a whole host of other negative, toxic things going on in my egoic mind and as a result, my body. What would it get me? Nothing really. Just the list of toxic feelings I mentioned poisoning my day. The smile comes from a victory. Not a victory over the other driver, but over myself—my egoic thinking. As far as the other driver? I feel sorry for them. They are carrying all of those negative, toxic feelings with them down the road, and that really sucks for them. This is an example of putting the "us" of driving into action. I can feel compassion for the other driver instead of resentment. As a result, I am acting compassionately toward myself. What a victory!

I had an experience where I was driving on the highway practicing awareness in the current moment. I was in the left-hand lane of a three-lane highway, and I wanted to move to the right into the middle lane. I checked my mirror and saw there was a black midsized sedan in the middle lane and it would not be safe to move over to the right until I had either let them drive by me or sped up enough to make some room for myself to get over to the right. I looked back ahead of me and then again to my passenger's side mirror in anticipation of making my move. It was then that I noticed the black car had moved into the far right lane of the three lanes and was moving past me, giving me ample room to move over. I put on my signal and started to move into the middle lane. I was startled by the honking, swerving black car in the middle lane that I had just completely cut off! I pulled back into the left lane and realized that the black car I had seen in the far right lane was a completely different black car. It looked very similar, and I thought to myself that anyone could have made the same mistake!

Because I was in my driving practice, I became aware of a valuable lesson learned in my present moment experience. Two, actually! One, check your mirror anyway. The car you see may not be same car you saw a few seconds ago. And two, everyone makes mistakes...including me! It was an honest mistake. I was paying attention. I wasn't on the phone or playing with the radio. In fact, I was practicing present moment driving awareness...I couldn't be paying more attention! And yet I made the mistake. I decided to make a mental note of that in my thinking mind so that when someone cut me off, I would realize that we all make mistakes. Then I could react with compassion rather than anger.

If you can admit the times when you have made mistakes when on the road, you can begin to learn to react differently when confronted with difficult situations presented by other drivers. By learning that to make a mistake is to be human, we can forgive others for being human in the present moment. By practicing unity with all humans and our environment, we can act with compassion and peace even though our first reaction might not be so serene. This is learning compassionate driving.

Instead of reacting with the thought, "That jerk just cut me off!" and the accompanying anger that goes with that line of thinking, take a step back and remove your ego from the equation. It might go something like this. "Someone made a mistake, and no one got hurt. We're all human. It is important to forgive others for being human and move on." What might have been a screaming tirade that produced plenty of toxic feelings and could have ignited into road rage is now just a small bump in the road. This puts us in harmony with the reality of the present moment.

Become the revolutionary evolutionary. Make the drive transformative. Find integration and unity and carry it with you. Make the way you enter your car different from the way you exit your car by centering, letting go, and dwelling in or as your higher self.

CHAPTER 12

GAINING INSIGHT

"A point of view can be a dangerous luxury when
substituted for insight and understanding."

— **Marshall McLuhan**

There are many benefits to developing a good driving practice. One of the chief benefits we have not yet touched on is gaining insight. A clear mind is an amazing tool for discovering that which your egoic mind blocks out. Often in my driving practice, when my mind is clear and I am coasting along the road in the present moment, an interesting phenomenon occurs. I have a realization. These realizations do not come from the thinking mind. So where do they come from? They come from the present moment and my attention to the experience of it. Some might say they come from God or from my higher self. To quantify or try to study this phenomenon only takes one further from the direct experience of it. It cannot be explained.

I can liken it to the muddy pond. When there is turbulence in the pond, the water is filled with debris and murky mud. This is emblematic of the egoic mind, murky in its thought patterns and turbulent with emotions, memories, and projections. One can see no further than the surface of the water and only guess at what lies beneath. Once the turbulence subsides and calm waters exist, the debris and mud sink to the bottom, revealing the transparent nature of the pond. Only then can the entirety of the pond be seen. This calm reveals what lies beneath the surface. It is an opportunity to see deeper. So it is with our minds. Once the debris and murkiness of the egoic mind subsides and calm is given a chance to take hold, the real, deeper nature of your being is revealed.

This real nature contains answers to many of the questions that are beyond the capacity of your thinking mind. They do not arise out of thought but rather are realized out of being. What that means is that there is no thought process by which you arrive at a solution. These realizations come more in the form of knowing and are beyond mind. This type of experience is actually the means by which I am writing this book.

I had been thinking about trying to use my time during my daily commute to improve my connection with my inner self and improve the attention I paid to the road while driving. I had tried to work on my connection with my higher-self using sitting meditation and had a little success. I learned that using the breath was a good bridge between the conscious mind and the unconscious mind. I then realized that driving can also be a bridge between the conscious and unconscious. We do it without any thought at all sometimes, but have the ability to bring our attention to it anytime. I had a fairly good idea that I might experience results if I tried to put a practice into action. Pretty noble endeavor. I had read several books on meditation, spirituality, and awareness and thought I would start with a few of the ideas I had gained along the way. At first, I had a hard time clearing away the egoic thought patterns that usually accompanied me on my commute, thoughts about the past, things that may be, abstract plans, or whatever emotional turmoil I was in at the time. As I relaxed more and refocused my attention on my driving experience, I noticed that I was having some success staying in the present moment with complete awareness.

As I continued to develop my practice over time, I noticed that I kept hearing about people's road rage experiences, distracted driving, and general dissatisfaction with their commute and their lives in general.

It was on a drive to work while I was experiencing the present moment with awareness when a "knowing" popped into my field of awareness that I might be able to help others achieve the calm, centered, present moment awareness that I was experiencing at that very moment. I felt in my gut that even if a few individuals were helped by a driving practice, it would be worth trying to get the message out. It was then that I started recording voice memos and making notes as the concepts and practices were exposed to me through presence in the moment.

I am not saying that these insights were a divine message. Only that they occurred to me through awareness in the present moment without a thought process. They were of my being, experience, and insight. Born in and of the moment. Nothing seemed more real or more right. This is the experience of insight in present moment awareness. What makes this insight so vital is that it is not clouded by the thinking, egoic mind.

When I decided to begin developing this practice not only for myself but so that it might help others to achieve a more serene, connected life and make for safer roads, my egoic mind hastily put up all sorts of roadblocks. I had thoughts of failure, self-doubt, and the thought of who was I to write about anything. Conversely, my egoic mind also painted a picture of grandeur. I would become a celebrated author, the newest self-help guru, and go on the talk show circuit. I was thankfully able to realize that this was all, for lack of a better term, bull. It was not the truth. It was a total fabrication of my ego. It was interesting for me to note, however, that my ego was playing both sides. Painting my efforts with only extreme highs and lows. That is how my ego works.

The reality is that there is no future for this writing. There is only the now. The now while I am typing these words. The now when I am developing my practice in my car. The now when I am listening to others talk about their experience on the road and in life. Only the now! My insight allowed me to see the truth, to recognize the truth about my egoic thinking mind and rely on the present moment to do the work. This was a great insight for me, as it can be for you.

"Should I send out my resume for that better job?" Don't listen to your self-doubt or your self-aggrandizement, just put it out there and let reality show you the truth.

"Should I ask that girl or guy out?" Don't let your self-doubt keep you from meeting the person you might have a really amazing connection with. I am not talking about being unrealistic with your expectations, I am talking about not having any expectations. If you can quiet your mind and be in the present moment, the insight will arise within you. It might not happen on your timetable, but it will happen if you are diligent in your practice.

The important insight I gained from this experience was that neither the egoic fear of not being good enough nor the egoic delusion of immediate total success and ultimate disillusionment should hold me back from exercising that which I feel is right in the current moment. Rather than *thinking* I wanted to start developing a driving practice and writing about it, I *knew* it was the right course of action for me. That course of action would be tested time and again by my egoic mind. My method was to acknowledge the ego and then move my awareness back to the present moment, thereby dissolving any conflict within me that the ego sought to create.

There is no inherent conflict in the reality of the now. The conflict is brought into being by the mind. One can argue that if someone is punching you in the face in the present moment, that is a conflict. Well, that doesn't mean much if you move away quickly or neutralize the attacker. You don't have to set up a conflict in your mind to act. Someone punches you in the now. You recognize what is happening. You take the appropriate steps to change the situation. Conflict is born of the mind and is usually the root of the violent act. It starts in the egoic, thinking mind until it finally manifests itself in an act of violence, harsh words, or is turned inward to manifest as depression and anxiety.

The egoic mind will seek to make everything a conflict...even things that don't exist. *Especially* things that don't exist. Don't believe the lie. The insight you gain through your practice may be that you begin to see the truth more and more. You become more awake to reality. You become aware of the reality of the present moment and experience it fully and completely. You connect with everything and everyone on a level plane and bring this insight into the world and the lives of others.

If something is troubling me, and it could even be my lack of perceived progress in my practice, I can set the intention at the start of my drive to gain insight into my situation. Often, while I am in the moment, a realization occurs within me that shines a light on the correct path of action (or inaction). This is similar to someone who prays for an answer.

I have heard it said that prayer is talking to God and meditation is listening to God. If you're not comfortable with the title God, that's fine. You can think of it as a Higher Power, the One Source, the Force, or whatever. It doesn't really matter how you label it, just that you give yourself a chance to experience it.

In my own practice, and from listening to others, I have found that the single greatest thing holding people back from realizing their true potential is fear. A driving practice can be a great tool for discovering the truth about yourself and your fear. Through your practice, certain truths are revealed to you on a gut level, the kinds of truth that you know to your deepest core are correct. One of these truths I have realized through my driving practice is that I am more than I think. Before I discovered the truth about myself (that I am much more than my thoughts), my life was ruled by fear. Looking back now, I can see so clearly how my false sense of self, which was ego based, was fragile, and easily fell victim to self-doubt and fear. I tried to think my way through life, ignoring the reality of what was right in front of me in the present moment. I felt confused, fearful, and lost. I was also in denial that I felt that way most of the time.

All of this mind manufactured fear, conflict, and helplessness brought about a certain feeling of being uncomfortable in my own skin. I believe that is why so many people turn to alcohol, drugs, gambling, and other addictive behavior—to relieve this feeling of being uncomfortable with life and uncomfortable as themselves. Most of us are just trying to cope with this general malaise using whatever means we can to avoid these feelings or at least garner a sense of hope that we can someday live happy and free.

I would set my attention on the future. Reaching a goal became the way that I coped with the fear. I told myself that once I achieved my goal, I would feel better, and the anxiety of life would leave me once and for all.

After reaching my goal, I was always disappointed that the elation was very short lived, and I was back in the same depressing spot...if not worse. I kept telling myself that it would get better... if only. If only I made more money, had more time, met better people, or whatever projection made me feel I had a chance. It was all a lie.

The insight I gained through living the pain of that lie, and then learning the truth through my practice, is that I didn't know who I really was. I was trying to satisfy this mental version of what

I thought it meant to be happy. I thought happy meant a lack challenges and perceived problems. That was never going to happen. To say I was being unrealistic would be an understatement. Unfortunately, a large portion of the population lives their lives in this way.

What was revealed to me through my practice was the truth—that I can only know my true self by experiencing, with complete awareness, the present moment. That is where my true self exists. In fact, it is the only place my true self exists. It is also the only place anything exists...including whatever your concept of God might be. The real me and my spiritual self are one and the same with all of life. Pretty heady stuff. But if kept out of the thinking mind and experienced directly, it is such a simple and acceptable truth that it changes lives. Some might call this a spiritual experience. I call it Truth.

It is important to note that my old way of thinking didn't just disappear at the realization of this Truth. I struggle, still experience anxiety, still catch myself becoming lost in my egoic thinking, and still feel lost sometimes. But I have realized that I have an option now. I can use the insights I have gained through my experience in practice to reset my course and experience Truth. That is why it is important to experience the present moment as often as possible. The more you practice, the more natural this way of experiencing your life becomes. The old habits are hard to break, and our egoic minds have been in charge since we became young adults. It is going to take time and determination in your practice to turn this around.

This, to me, is the highest endeavor one can pursue. The realization of Truth. Let your car and your practice be your vehicle.

CHAPTER 13

CARRYING YOUR DRIVING INTO OTHER LANES OF YOUR LIFE

"Meditation is a microcosm, a model, a mirror. The skills we practice when we sit are transferable to the rest of our lives."

— Sharon Salzberg

So what of this practice, the insights gained, and the experience of the Truth? How does this change my world...our world? I can't stay in my car forever.

The insights gained by practicing present moment awareness while driving may change your life. They may reaffirm what you have already felt at other times in your life. Your practice will serve as a reminder to you on a daily basis that you are your higher self. I try to bring that out into the world when I turn off my engine and get out of the car. I try to walk in life as my higher self, and my driving practice is my opportunity to refresh that realization several times a day.

I turn off my engine, set my intention to leave the car as my higher self, bring my attention into the now, and step forth into the world. My path is the sound of my feet upon the ground. Practicing PRND outside of the car is perfectly acceptable and, in fact, recommended. This is how you bring your practice with you out into the world, and you will see a world of difference.

Just as successful meditators cannot live their lives on the cushion, if you are practicing driving in awareness of the present moment, it is important that you bring the experience you witness with you out into the world. Yes, the way you drive will change. You will be much more aware of the other drivers on the road, drive with a greater sense of cooperation and compassion, and be more aware of the realities of driving in an environment where egoic thinking can transform itself into competition and road rage. But what else?

The change does not occur in your car, it occurs in yourself. If you are mindful only while driving, you will reap the benefits of a more centered and serene driving experience. But if you can learn to practice what you have experienced while driving out in the world, you can transform your life. If you can replace driving with walking, typing, reading, speaking, working, or any other part of your life, this transformation will grow. Once you experience the now directly, you can learn to experience life in the now anytime. All it takes is intention, relaxation, and bringing your attention into the now—just like in your car.

If you experience a sense of cooperation and compassion on the road, you can experience the same sense of higher self while shopping, waiting in line, or even dealing with your children or family. These scenarios may require some adjustment and effort, but if the seeds of Truth are firmly planted in your experience through your driving practice, you can make transformation happen. It is through the repeated efforts of your driving practice that you are able to reach deeper and more meaningful experiences while driving down the road. Why not take these same efforts with you down the road of life?

Let's take waiting in line as an example. Generally, people hate waiting in line. It is akin to being stuck in traffic. (Some of the greatest experiences in my driving practice have happened while I have been stuck in traffic.) First notice your feet on the ground as you stand in the line. Realize that you are in a line and that lines can move slowly and take longer than you would like. This is a fact. Surrender to that fact. Set your intention to use this time in line to not let your egoic mind run wild with rage and anxiety, to not shift constantly and look ahead in the line, sighing and shaking your head. This will not change the amount of time you will have to wait, it will only make your experience awful. People tend to take these feelings with them when they leave the line and go back out into the world. That would be quite unfortunate and unnecessary.

Instead, set your attention to use this situation to work on your present moment awareness. In Zen Buddhism, there is a walking meditation called kinhin. It is practiced in the Zendo between long periods of zazen, or sitting meditation. I have practiced zazen in the Zendo, and let me tell you, kinhin is a welcome break after sitting in silence for a long period of time. Everyone rises from their cushion and walks in lockstep, their hands together in front of them, with a loose gaze at the floor in front of their feet. We walked in serpentine fashion around the Zendo with our intention to keep our awareness on our walking. Our path was the feeling of our feet upon the ground. We experience the current moment with awareness.

So feel your feet on the ground, notice your breathing while you stand there, look around and notice the other people in line, experience the now of standing in line. If your attention gets distracted by your egoic, thinking mind, bring your attention back to the breath, your feet, the line, the present reality of where you are in the moment. Keep checking your body to make sure you are relaxed, scan your shoulders and neck to release any tension.

Your ego will try to hijack the experience of waiting in line. It is our human condition. Thoughts may pop up that will distract you from the reality of the present moment. These egoic thoughts seek to motivate you to deny the reality of the present moment. They seek to add emotion, fear, and anxiety to the experience for you. They steal your attention.

For me, my egoic mind takes a look at the situation and immediately seeks to deny the reality that I am simply waiting in line. A thought may enter my field of attention that tells me this isn't fair, this is a waste of my valuable time, how dare they make ME wait in line, there should be more people working here, and so on ad nauseum. This is not the truth.

It has the effect of snowballing and raising emotions in me that will manifest in my body. I will become tense, jittery, and angry. My body will give the emotions life by shifting my feet, tightening my shoulders and neck muscles, making my breathing more shallow and quick. If I have the presence of mind gained from my driving practice to recognize that I am falling into my ego's trap, I can act. I know from experience that if I try not to think the thoughts that my ego is creating, I will only give them more power. I also know that if I set my intention to practice present moment awareness, check my body for tension, and relax, gently bringing my attention into the now and practice, the egoic hold on me will collapse on itself and dissolve. The simple moment it takes to use PRND can transform my whole experience. I may have to do that several times while in line, just like I do while driving, but it works every time.

If you have an experience like this you will begin to notice that the anxiety of waiting in line only existed in your own mind. The manifestations of that anxiety melt away in the light of present moment awareness. You may even catch yourself smiling as you realize you are standing in line totally unannoyed. Bring yourself back to the present moment awareness of your higher self experiencing waiting in a line. The alternative of standing there as an angry, annoyed bundle of tightly wound nerves is no way to live. Once you experience Truth, it gives you a certain sense of serenity and calm. Hopefully, you will take this with you after waiting in line, out into the world.

If you begin to employ what you have learned and your experiences in your practice to your life in general, you will notice a transformation taking place. You will begin to realize that you have a choice, a conscious choice, when it comes to how you want to live your life. You can choose to live awake! At any moment, you can become aware in the present moment and live the Truth. The more you experience the liberation of Truth, the more you will recognize its absence. You will notice when your ego is trying to hijack your attention and be able to act.

It is important to realize that no one is perfect. At times, your ego will get the upper hand...for a while. Remember, we are comfortable with the uncomfortable feelings and thoughts that we have become used to from our years of egoic thinking. It takes diligent practice to bring about change. I catch myself feeding into my old egoic ways and pause. I say to myself, "I don't need to do this." Then I reset my attention and right the ship. Liberation!

Mornings can be a particularly tough time for me to be in the moment. Often, when I wake up in the morning, I am still tired. I am not one of those people who springs out of bed ready to devour the day. I am more the ramp up kind of person. My mind tends to be a bit sluggish when I first get out of bed, and I can easily fall into egoic thinking. I am projecting about my day, feeling like I could use a few more minutes of sleep, thinking about the upcoming weekend, and just generally in a funk. If I have the presence of mind to change that, I can have a great start to the day.

I start with brushing my teeth. I can put a post-it note on the mirror to remind myself to practice PRND. (Or I might just put the letters PRNB on the note. Practice, Relax, Now, Brush.) I can feel the brush in my hand, the tube of toothpaste squeezing while the paste comes out, the taste of mint, the feel of the brush. I take in the whole experience without thought, judgment, or projection.

I turn on the shower and feel the water, the temperature, my feet on the floor, the smell of the soap. It is odd to think it, but I am really taking a shower. Before developing my practice, I would have missed the whole experience while I projected in my mind the entire time. Instead, I can start the day with the calm and serenity of knowing and experiencing the truth of myself in the present moment and take that out into the world. Simple, but not easy. Notes can help. I have a friend who is a big believer in reminder notes. He puts them on his mirror and in his car, and they work for him. If you have time, you can read something spiritual first thing in the morning. This can set you on the right track to start your day. Try a few things if you need a little reminder or jump-start. Find the things that work for you and use them. We all need a little help sometimes. Why not help yourself?

⊷⊶ ⊷⊶

You are also going to find situations that are particularly tough for you to practice present moment awareness in. These are usually times that have the potential to be highly charged with emotion. Dealing with family situations, conflicts, people, and personality issues—things that push our buttons. If you can pause when you feel the tension rising in your body and stop your mind for a moment, let go of the tension, step back, and reassess the situation, examine the reality of the problem, and attempt to approach your part in it as your higher self, this can change everything. Usually, situations that ramp up quickly have their origins in feelings of fear. Fear can quickly manifest itself as anger, anxiety, and even violence. Taking the time to pause and reassess from a higher point of view can go a long way toward de-escalating a situation and bringing a conflict back down to a manageable level. It is in situations like this that we can learn a lot about ourselves and our practice.

The more you practice, the more easily and quickly you will recognize when you are becoming out of balance. When your awareness tells you that you are slipping into an egoic state, it is necessary to step back and reset. The more you bring your practice into other parts of your day besides your driving, the more your higher self will manifest in your everyday life. It is important to keep on with your driving practice as you build your practice in other areas of your life. The driving practice is your sanctuary away from a lot of other distractions. It is also where you got your start, and the familiarity of practicing while driving may make it easier to connect with the present moment for you.

You may also notice that as you allow present moment awareness to enter your life, you become more creative, more motivated to explore new things, and less afraid of things that used to cause you worry and anxiety. Once you open up to Truth, life seems less frightening, more boundless, and much more serene. I noticed that when I felt myself getting out balance, I could call upon my practice and get back to reality. My balance was being upset by my own mind. By refocusing on what was real and truthful, I could feel the anxiety lose its power.

The more I shared about what I had experienced, the more I came to the realization that since I couldn't give the experience to anyone with my words, it was hard if not impossible to share any meaningful truth of the experience with anyone unless they were open to it already. I remember trying to discuss the benefits of what I had learned with someone and they began to refute the basics of my experience with words. They argued that the past and future did indeed exist right now and that my intellect was indeed my reality. I found it to be like trying to change someone's mind about politics—probably not going to happen. I also realized that it was OK that life is set up that way. Those of you who read this work may indeed be ready to try to practice and have a transformative experience. There are others who will read the same work and walk away from it unconvinced that it is worth a try.

In other words, if you don't want it, it will not be there for you. If you want it, it will. It isn't necessarily there for those who need it, just for those who want it. It requires an open mind, a teachable demeanor, and an attitude of discovery. So do not be discouraged if you have success and want to share it with others but they are not receptive. It is not a concrete object you can share with them; it is an experience on a most personal level. If we have that experience in common, we can all share about it. If we are speaking about it with someone who has not shared the experience, or who is not at least willing to be open to it, they are not going to be receptive. That is OK. Keep practicing, and your example will serve as a beacon to those who need relief from the egoic, thinking mind.

I have found that the more I practice, the experience of practice becomes second nature to me. I can get into my car, quickly PRND, and get into the present moment with awareness. Distractions are overcome more easily with experience, and I am able to carry my present moment awareness with me out into the world with less effort. These are the benefits of a diligent practice. In this way, your higher self becomes better integrated into your conscious life, and you are able to live a more serene, connected existence. This new way of life leads to a more fulfilling, compassionate, and confident way of being. I feel as though I am awake. I can also more easily feel when I am not awake and take the steps necessary to open myself back up to the present moment Truth.

By "not awake," I mean that I am in the egoic mental state of clock time, competition with the world, and disconnectedness. A world of paradoxes, opposites, and opposing forces. In the reality of the present moment, the non-egoic world of the higher self, I awake to Truth of an existence that transcends the egoic world of the mind. This is the freedom of true existence that practice can unlock. I am free of my sense of self that is separate from everything.

When I carry that awareness out into the world, I notice several things change immediately. First, I am definitely more physically relaxed. My anxiety level is way down; I feel more at ease because I am connected to everything. My level of fear is greatly diminished as I move through the world being an integral part of the ongoing unfolding of creation. I am one. I am flexible. Instead of fighting my way through life, I am flowing with life. I have surrendered to Truth.

I also notice that my interactions with others are far more compassionate than they were previously. I am more forgiving, less judgmental, and generally more accepting of the people I come in contact with. I also spend less energy comparing myself to everyone else...what a relief. Since I am spending less mental energy spinning my wheels in my egoic mind, I have more focus and clarity in my awareness of the present moment. I am mentally sharper when life calls upon me to use my intellect to make a decision or choose a path. I am using my intellect, not falling victim to it. I am realizing that my intellect is my most valuable tool for survival, not who I am. I am a spiritual being having a human experience.

⊷✢✦

When I am awake in the present moment, I am clear. I am not encumbered by the constant barrage of thoughts, projections, and memories. I more instinctively know how to act in any given situation. I am no longer running away, seeking relief, or fearing boredom. This is true freedom.

In order to find this freedom, I can look in the most mundane of places. Simple tasks that I considered part of the boring routine that was life. Brushing my teeth, taking a shower, waiting in line, and of course, driving. Seek out these mundane tasks in your life and make them a starting point for practicing present moment awareness. They are usually a great gateway to the now that can easily be accessed on a daily basis. It is a great opportunity to extend your practice outside of your car.

Above all else, give yourself a chance to practice wherever and whenever possible. At first, it may seem like you are spending all of your waking moments trying to push yourself into your practice. It is definitely going to take intention and effort to break the bonds of the egoic thinking patterns we have lived with since our childhood. These patterns are deep within our minds and bodies and aren't going to change without some real work. It is important to keep this in mind if you are going to find freedom from self and realize Truth in your life. The change will come slowly, but it will come. You will notice small changes and also some setbacks. Keep your focus only on your practice, not on the immediate results. Change will come!

For me, this is my life's work. The answer to the question that at one time seemed unanswerable. To live the Truth.

CHAPTER 14

UNITY IN THE NOW

*"All differences in this world are of degree, and not of
kind, because oneness is the secret of everything."*

— Swami Vivekananda

O nce you develop a consistent driving practice, are able to
connect to the current moment with awareness and be present in the now, and have also experienced that presence in other
parts of your life outside of the car, you are in a position to integrate your experiences, knowledge, and practice into a way of being. A unity that is about bringing together our intelligent mind,
body, and spirit in order to live a better life, make better decisions,
and practice self-examination.

Your unified integration can become your source for the current moment Truth that will become your compass. You can make
better decisions, free of ego, fear, and false judgment. Your personal relationships can be filled with compassion, understanding, and
love. Most of all, your inward experience will be transformed. This

transformation results in your outward experiences being transformed as well. Eastern traditions call this enlightenment.

Since you are human, this enlightenment is neither permanent nor complete. It takes ongoing effort, practice, and keen awareness of self and the world around you. There is no graduation from this practice. In order to live as an aware being, you must practice as an aware being. There will always be the natural ups and downs of life. It is how these are experienced and dealt with that is the deciding difference between living a life of quiet desperation and a life of freedom from self and delusion. If you live the Truth, you will be the Truth. But again, as we are human, we will not be perfect at it.

One thing I have learned from my practice is to make decisions and problem solve while keeping my awareness in the now. I use my intelligent mind as it was intended to be used to lead a serene and compassionate life. I have learned to recognize what is real and what is my egoic mind's interpretation of what is real. This becomes second nature as a practice develops.

If I find that I am at a crossroads and need to make a decision as to which way to go, but am not sure, I can offer the circumstances up to the current moment awareness and examine the situation with care and compassion. Instead of being motivated by fear, greed, lust, or any other ego-manufactured feelings, I can shine the light of Truth on myself and make decisions with clarity, conviction, and faith. I can examine the circumstances, recognize any egoic influences and interpretations, and let those fall away. I can then bring my focus back to the present moment and observe a clear view of the truth of the situation. It may not come immediately; it may take several tries to see clearly. But eventually, Truth reveals itself.

I know that I will feel the ego trying to creep in and influence the way I think and feel about the circumstances, but these are easily recognized and attention is brought back to the reality of the present moment awareness. Often, the decision is quite mundane, and sometimes, it is so bold that I must reexamine it because my self-doubt is so strong. This is where faith comes in. I have to have faith in the truth of my current moment awareness. I have to take the step of not knowing and be confident in myself, my practice, and Truth. It also means that I accept it may not work out the way I think it is going to, but it will work out the way the universe intended. This is where true faith is tested. Your experience of Truth must be strong enough that you can surrender to it and accept the path it presents before you. This takes not only faith but strength, the strength to recognize self-doubt and fear and examine them under the light of present moment awareness. Strength to not give in to the old way of thinking, the egoic mind's version of reality. The strength to get out of your comfort zone to experience real growth.

This strength will take courage. The courage to live in the Truth when your ego is nagging at you to return to the safety of delusion, a deluded way of thinking where you can decide what is real and what isn't and safely spin the truth to delude yourself into a false self-confidence. Through your experience, you will know that this is the false reality that caused you to live your life in detached uneasiness and desperation. There is no desperation in Truth. Your strength and courage will be tested over and over again. The good news is, when you experience your strength and courage as an integral part of Truth, your ego will lose strength as it is revealed to be a weakness that was holding you back from Truth. Your ego has been telling you that you can't handle the Truth. Your courage and strength will reveal that not only *can* you handle it, but you don't want to live without it. Any other way of being would be a lie.

It will also take courage and strength to learn to wait...patience. We are used to taking action immediately when we feel uncomfortable with a situation. Sometimes, the prudent course of action dictates that we wait. This can be more difficult than acting. We are nagged by worry as we are not confident that things will work out as we had hoped. This nagging anxiety and worry make life difficult and uncomfortable. These are all manifestations of the ego and are not Truth. Dealing with the discomfort of waiting is quite a challenge without faith, courage, and strength. If we can learn to surrender to the truth of the present moment, accept that the unfolding reality that is now will not lead us down a wrong path, and trust ourselves and our practice, we can learn patience and live a serene and honest life.

These qualities of faith, courage, and strength must be cultivated, learned, and relearned. They are an affirmation that you believe in Truth and are living in the now with awareness and presence. Trusting the Truth of the universe is a very difficult thing for us to do. Without constant examination and reexamination, this Truth is not even recognizable. When this is the case, we rely only on our ego and our thinking to make our way in the world. This is what has led us to the unhappiness of living in an egoic state.

Reexamination of ourselves without egoic influences is not judgment or criticism; it is simply seeing ourselves for what we are and gently guiding our behaviors back to the Truth. It is a moment to pause and look at our lives. This is a time to reflect and take a look at our thoughts and actions and examine them under the light of Truth and then make the necessary adjustments in our practice to keep us on the path. We can look at our compassion, openness, and acceptance. We can examine relationships, attitudes, conflicts, and feelings and see where we detect our old egoic ways influencing our lives. It is important that this self-examination take place in the light of current moment awareness and Truth. It is an exercise of the intelligent mind and can easily slip into egoic influences. These influences of the ego (fear, anger, etc.) can be recognized for what they are and our attention brought back to Truth. This requires a quiet space in our lives, the right mindset, and an openness with Truth. We must be able to accept our mistakes and move past them, learn from them, and forgive ourselves and others for not being perfect. We can say we are sorry and make amends to those we have wronged with our egoic words and actions.

Our first inclination will be to blame others for our circumstances. Our ego will make excuses that seek to clear us of any wrongdoing. If we can examine our part in the situation, we can begin to make positive changes in ourselves and the parts of our conflicts that we can control. In other words, we have to realize that we are powerless over others and act on ourselves to effect change. We learn to look at the behavior of others as something that we can accept and then respond to or choose to not respond at all. If we react in our old usual ways, we are giving power to not only our ego but theirs as well. This is how situations can escalate very quickly into something that is extremely toxic. Our ego needs to be right—and so does theirs. As this battle of the egos ramps up, it gets uglier and nastier.

This can be defused by removing your ego from the equation. By recognizing their ego, you can remove the influence of your ego and change the entire dynamic. This does not mean that you will be their doormat. It simply means you will decide not to play the ego game anymore. You can end the conversation, walk away, or simply agree to disagree. As you feel your toxic energy ramping up, let this be your signal to take a step back, relax, and consciously remove your ego from the exchange. It can work wonders.

You can make alerting yourself to the signals of a toxic situation part of your practice. By being alert and aware in the present moment in any situation, you can practice your exploration of Truth. This Truth is seen mostly in yourself, but also in the behavior of others. You can recognize in them that which you have experienced. You can empathize with their frustrations and fears because you have learned to recognize them in yourself. This empathy leads to compassion. Rather than firing back at a harsh verbal attack, you can learn to step back and recognize the feelings of fear and anger in someone else, knowing you have been there yourself. Their perspective will change when you offer some understanding to them instead of what they are expecting—someone hitting them back. You're not telling them they're right or wrong, just that you have felt like that before and can understand feelings of frustration and anger. Sometimes, that is all that is needed to defuse a toxic situation. Your practice with these types of encounters can lead to a deeper understanding of yourself and others.

Witnessing the mechanisms of the ego in your practice and then in others is a great way to integrate your practice into the world. It creates compassion in you and can open the door for others to learn compassion as well. What a beautiful thing! If you can deal with others with integrity, honesty, and openness, there are few who will not have a positive experience interacting with you.

There are always some who will see these admirable character traits as disingenuous or as an opportunity to take advantage of someone who is naïve. These individuals are easily recognizable because you have seen their motivations in your own past egoic thinking. By remaining steadfast in your practice and in your present moment awareness, you will become aware of their toxicity very quickly and act to defuse their egoic influence over the situation or conversation with understanding and Truth. These are the types of egoic thinkers who use words as weapons and deception as truth. Often it is best to not engage these individuals in lengthy debate, but rather quickly and politely remove yourself and limit your exposure to their toxicity. Life is too short!

It is also important to take care of yourself physically. Eating healthy, exercising, challenging your intellect, and resting well can all go a long way to integrating your practice into a healthy lifestyle and a serene life. Although these seem obvious components to a happy, healthy life, our ego can tell us that we are different from everyone else and can get by on less sleep, junk food, or a lot of TV better than the average person. Use your practice to recognize your egoic thinking in your motivations. The ego can tell you that you deserve to be lazy and spend the day on the couch watching TV and eating junk food. Make the examination of your motivations an important part of your practice. Once you are in touch with the Truth in the present moment, you can tap into it in every aspect of your life to live better and think clearer.

Fear can keep you from going to the gym to work out. Anger can make you binge eat junk food. Self-loathing can keep you from getting out of bed in the morning, and so on. These emotional feelings can hold us hostage as long as we allow the ego to run our lives. Your driving practice is the start to recognizing that we are not our thoughts, we are the ones who witness our thoughts. We are also the ones who can choose to practice so we can recognize them and shift the power away from them and to the present moment and the Truth contained therein. That is where freedom from self can begin.

By checking our motivations, we can discover the root of what is holding us back from the life we ideally would like to be leading. We can use our practice and our discovery of Truth to change everything about ourselves and the way we act. We can build a strong, healthy body, a sharp, curious mind, and an active social life with people we love. By opening the door to Truth with our practice, we have the opportunity to better ourselves and the world.

CHAPTER 15

BON VOYAGE

"No one saves us but ourselves. No one can and no one may. We ourselves must walk the path."

— Buddha

The French phrase bon voyage literally means "good journey," and this is what we hope to create—a good journey—for your drive and your life. By developing a driving practice of current moment awareness, we are making our way toward a safer, more serene, and more compassionate experience on the road. By cultivating the Truth in our present moment awareness and reducing or eliminating our egoic way of thinking and driving, we can practice a better way of being while we drive and while we live.

We develop a sense of cooperation with other drivers, traffic, and the journey. By making contact with our serene, higher self, we all but eliminate the anger that can spiral into road rage or other forms of unsafe, aggressive driving. By making our driving safer, we in turn make the road a little bit safer for everyone, and that is a very good thing indeed. We can defuse potentially dangerous situations that are based on anger and ego before they get out of hand. All of this is of great benefit to others on the road, certainly, but is of especially great benefit to ourselves. We learn to give ourselves a break and also learn to forgive others on the road.

Once you experience the change in the way you feel and act in the car through your practice, you will remain motivated to keep your practice fresh and extend your new way of experiencing the now into other areas of your life. Your driving practice can really bring about a "good journey" every time you get into the driver's seat, no matter what the particular circumstances of your situation on any given day. The car will become your laboratory, a place where you can experiment with your perceptions of yourself, others, and the world in general, finding out for yourself what is Truth and what is not.

The voyage of awareness can continue when you get out of your car and walk in the outside world. Your life can take on a new way of being, with a realistic outlook free of egoic fear and anxiety, free of anger and outrage, free of delusion and self-doubt. It all springs from your practice! What starts as something you read about and decided to try while you drove one day can be the seed that changes everything for you…if you want it to. All it takes is an open mind and a little commitment to practice. You have nothing to lose and everything to gain.

Even if you get away from your practice for a day, a month, or a year, all it takes is getting in the car and seeing that PRND on your dashboard. The only time to practice is now. It is the only time you ever can practice, so don't let perceived failures keep you from Truth. Set your intention to practice. Relax. Bring your attention into the now. And drive. It really is that simple.

For me, my car and my commute to and from work every day have become something I can look forward to. It is my time to reset and rejuvenate. No matter how I am feeling when I get into my car, I know that it is within my power to work toward revealing the Truth in the current moment and letting the light of that Truth warm my spirit and renew my serenity. What a great gift to myself.

That being said, it is not always my first thought. My ego would rather go off on a rampage or a dream or a deluded conversation with myself than take a back seat to the current moment and the Truth of reality. No matter how much time I have spent in practice, I must always be vigilant of my ego and its power over my thinking. I have to remember that the power of my choice must come from beyond ego. If I can remember this, I will not be fooled and can walk (or drive) the path (or road) of Truth.

It is valuable to remember that your practice will be tested time and time again. Circumstances will present themselves that would normally be a hot button for your ego to react and take over. If your presence is strong in the Truth of the current moment, this can be prevented. Even if your ego has already started its reaction, you can pull back, pause, and reset your intention to practice in this environment. If you do, it will become abundantly clear to you that you have made the right move. How? You can notice a serenity that you would not normally find in an intense situation. You can notice a lack of toxic feelings in your body and the absence of their corresponding tension.

These tests are what reveal to us the Truth of our new way of being. These victories let us know that we are on the right path. When we sense growth in ourselves, it may also be noticed by others. We may find our friends and families coming to us in their hour of need. That may test us even further, but is a great gift if we practice with diligence and compassion. Some may even ask us what our secret is.

The secret is...there is no secret. We are only acting from the Truth of the present moment with presence, awareness, and compassion. Usually, when I tell someone about this, they give me a very strange look. If they have never heard of these concepts before, they are quite taken aback by my words. They may ask me if I am talking about God. I usually respond with, "Something like that." It is hard to explain to someone who either has no experience with the Truth of current moment awareness or has a set religious belief system that they may feel is threatened by these concepts.

Since what I am talking about is largely experiential, explaining it is very difficult. Some who may have had experiences in meditation, Eastern thought, or spiritual philosophy may be able to demonstrate a better degree of understanding and acceptance of the concepts of Truth. But without the benefit of direct experience through practice, it is of little practical value to others except maybe to give them a direction to seek out their own practice and experiences. By trying to explain this, you may put yourself out there as an oddball. Fear not! I believe we will all arrive at Truth eventually. So don't be afraid to be a pioneer...a revolutionary evolutionary...an oddball.

Sharing the gift of Truth is a great thing, but must be approached with much care and skill. You really can't give it to someone who doesn't want it. You also can't give it with just words. You really can't give it at all. The other person has to take it—every bit of it—themselves. If it isn't their own, it will never be at all. Think of your own experience. If you don't experience the unseen Truth for yourself, can you ever truly believe in it or put it into practice for yourself? I know I can't.

For me, it has to be tested and retested and retested again. Then it becomes Truth to me. After that, it is obvious to me that it always was and always will be Truth. But I have to remember back to how it was before I experienced it directly. I have to put myself back into their shoes and see it from their perspective.

It is important to not push too hard. A simple suggestion can go a long way. Suggest that they read about it or try a simple exercise in their car for themselves. Maybe give them a copy of this book and let them figure it out for themselves. Just tell them about your experience with your practice and let them take from it what works for them. After all, that is all I am really doing with this book. I am laying out what I have found in hopes you may find something in it that helps you find Truth for yourself. You can do the same.

It is not a good idea to evangelize or seek to convert others to your new way of being. It is much better to set an example, and if asked, share as much as they are willing to take. Be a willing mentor if that is what they would like. It can be very rewarding. Discuss your own experiences and share your own stories. The important thing is to share without expectation. Don't take it personally if people tell you it sounds like a lot of esoteric bull. They are right. If it isn't experienced directly, it *is* just a bunch of words that mean a lot to you because you know their Truth, but to them, are just concepts that are seen only by their egoic mind. That egoic mind sees the concepts as unrealistic and a fantasy. Only their higher self will ever be able to recognize Truth.

Do not be discouraged. Do not push. Do not be hurt by rejection of the concepts you hold dear. These are all feelings that originate in the ego. If you take a moment and look at their reaction in the light of Truth, you can take refuge in the fact that whether they experience it or not, whether they like it or not, or even whether they think you are nuts or not, you know your Truth. So let Truth do its work. Let Truth find its own way. All we can do is be present in the moment with complete awareness and live our lives in the Truth. Like I said before, we will all arrive at Truth eventually.

I would like to remind you to be kind to yourself as well. We as humans tend to push ourselves when we feel we are not getting or giving enough to achieve our goals. Remember that there is no ultimate goal in your practice. The only goal is to practice. If you feel that you are not progressing fast enough or are wasting your time, remember that the origin of these feelings and thoughts is your ego. Remember that your egoic mind will seek to derail your practice. It's not like there is some other being named "ego" living inside you. It is just that your intellect has been hijacked by the phenomenon of ego, and one mechanism of this phenomenon is that your ego develops its own sense of identity and tells you that it is who you are. Through your practice, you find out this is not the case, but your ego doesn't just go away. It will always be there as a phenomenon of the mind that has been developed over thousands of years. Do not be deterred by it; it is dissolved in the light of the Truth of the current moment.

If you are feeling self-doubt about your practice, just PRND and keep on being. The choice you have is to ignore Truth and live as an egoic being or spearhead this change within yourself and mankind to recognize the Truth of who and what you really are— your higher self. Remember that this endeavor takes courage and perseverance, acceptance and surrender, strength and wisdom. Whatever you don't have of these when you start your practice, you can pick up along the way. That is one of the benefits of practice.

Be always aware that you are human. You are a spiritual being having a human experience. Before the light of Truth reveals that to you, you may feel like a human being who occasionally has a spiritual experience. For some, it is their belief that they are human, period. There is no spirit. No truth. Just their intellect, ego, and body. For me, that seems like a pretty bleak existence. From my experience, I also know it is not true for me. I can't speak to their truth, nor is it my place to. I can only know Truth through my own existence.

Though a community of like-minded people may come into existence as it relates to practice, Truth, and our journey, it is not necessary for developing a practice. It might make it easier in some sense, but it also comes with other problems of ego, competition, and conflict. The base of a practice will always remain within the individual. I alone am responsible for the development of my practice and the Truth that may be revealed to me through it. I am the only one who can ultimately know my Truth because I am the only one who has experienced it as I have. This may sound like a lonely road. It is not.

As your practice develops, it opens up the whole world to you. You connect with everything and everyone. You will not do it perfectly (no one does), but you will feel this sense of connection as you experience Truth in current moment awareness. The Truth shall set you free. Free from what? From yourself, yourself as it was contained in your egoic, thinking mind. Yourself as it was experienced through the ego as self-doubt, fear, and anger. The Truth will reveal to you the Real You, your higher self as you are meant to be. That is the gift of practice.

It is truly a life's work...our life's work, experienced one moment at a time. That is the only true way it can be experienced.

Remember that when traveling down the road of life, there is no ultimate destination. It truly is about the journey. If there is a destination, it is only the current moment. Since our egoic, thinking mind can only conceive of a destination as an ending, and the current moment has no end (and no beginning), it serves to really confuse the thinking mind. So go forward with your practice, and enjoy the journey. Bon voyage!

CPSIA information can be obtained
at www.ICGtesting.com
Printed in the USA
FSHW021105051218
54257FS